MADBiz Asia Solutions
Delivering the *Difference* in
Your Business Results

A result-focused business improvement and
team development consulting firm.

*What they
say about*
MADBiz

"The
Mad
Culture"

WESTBOW
PRESS
A DIVISION OF THOMAS NELSON

D. Lauren's book applies a distinctly Asian perspective to organizational and customer management, culture, and change. It introduces a combination of **MADBiz** methods of motivation, leadership, sales force development, and personal improvement to effect successful culture change. I enjoyed the specific examples on the implementation of **MAD** values, particularly the anecdotal evidence of the results it delivered.

The book provides insight into the techniques of creating and realizing a performance improvement culture for organizations. The measurement of the tangible benefits resulting from culture change remains one of the most exigent topics in change management literature.

— *Jason Seng,*
   Senior Consultant in Strategy and Change, London. Co-author,
   Making Change Work: Closing the Change Gap, Human Resource
   International Management Digest

In *The MAD Culture*, D. Lauren reveals how to strengthen relationships with employees and customers to increase business performance and profitability.

Based on her extensive experience building brands and managing organizational change, D. Lauren provides detailed guidance on inspiring oneself and others to achieve peak performance — no matter what the work climate is. Packed with guidance on creating a winning team together to achieve desired results, she offers concrete steps for making a difference in any workplace.

It takes more to stand out in today's cluttered marketplace, but fostering a positive culture and behavior is vital for any organizational success. **MADBiz** helps you bridge the gap so you can get more out of every business and customer opportunity.

— *T Cecilia,*
   Global Marketing Knowledge Manager, London

What they say about
"The MAD Culture"

The sad truth about organizations that fail to progress is that they are led by leaders who play it safe with a "if it ain't broken, why fix it" mentality. Then there are those who sit by the side — apportioning blame in failure yet quick to claim credit for success. The old saying that "the fish stinks from the head" is true in real life. Success of an organization essentially rests with the leader who is capable of making decisions and who can motivate both staff and customers into a win-win situation for mutual benefit.

Business and management titles found in regular bookstores are by tycoons or management gurus who manage big businesses with billion-dollar turnovers. However, these books may not be relevant to the small and medium-sized enterprises.

MADBiz readers will find that they can boldly apply the contents of this book into their business practice, no matter the size of their organizations.

This book exemplifies a leader who dared to make the difference and had the courage to endure short term pains for long term gains without running down the competition. I am confident that many, like me, will find D. Lauren's ideas, thought provoking and inspiring.

— *R.Goh,*
   recipient of the Lifetime Achievement Award in the 2007 World Gourmet Summit and the Outstanding Leadership Award 2006-7 at the Hospitality Asia Platinum Excellence Awards.

MADBiz : The MAD Culture is a book that will awaken the thinking of an executive who has gotten used to doing the same things because it either worked in the past or the status quo does not affect the unit he is managing. It challenges one to think globally rather than parochially. In an organization where people have got used to going with the flow, the new way of doing things will really be met by resistance, especially by those who can't adapt to the changes.

This book basically teaches an executive on how to handle cultural transformation. While an idea may be good and proper, failure to effect the changes will occur if the people will not respond to it or there is weakness in implementation. It also tackles the choice of the right people to make sure that everything will work as planned. Those who can't go on must give way or be cut out of the team. While they may be competent people, the author of this book also warns that competency is not enough. People must also have the right character.

The MAD Culture is a valuable piece of work for every manager in the field, as it shakes one's thinking process on people, the links in the organization, the existing tools and systems, and other issues. This can form pieces that can lead to knowing what must be done to achieve the business goals as a first step, the courage and will to implement it as the second, the right people to do it as third, and the passion and clear direction of the leadership to make it work and influence the troops to winning as the most important of all.

— *R. Geneblazo,*
  Vice President, Sterling Bank of Asia, The Philippines

I was greatly enlightened when I read about the turnaround business that is all about having the right strategy, the right timing, and the right execution. Many failures are results of poor execution. It struck me, as I am currently managing a turnaround business.

The MAD Culture reminds me that I need to realign my focus, look within the organization for talent, and coach and guide the people to bring out the best in them. It is really important for people to know the core values of the organization and to adhere to it at all costs, for at the end of the day, that is what it takes to achieve great accomplishments. The **MAD** strategies on "create, leverage, differentiate, and dominate" have helped me to keep thinking on the questions I need to ask myself: how to set challenging growth goals; how to create, orchestrate, and promote the team to a high standard of performance; how to focus and strategize on differentiating points to lead in the targeted product categories, brands, segmentations, or channels.

In any organization, one must always think he/she is important to the company, expect outstanding results, and go beyond meeting customers' expectations. Leading change must start from oneself, and it is wrong to wait for someone to enforce you to adapt to the change. As the saying goes, "Time to change" and time for growth will follow.

This book is very enlightening. It makes you pause, reflect, and think!

— *G. Ederine,*
Managing Director, Rentokil Initial Philippines

What they say about
"The MAD Culture"

MADBiz : **The MAD Culture** is an excellent book. Rarely do I start a book and not stop before finishing it. This is one of the books that I find it to be so captivating and real, and I can relate so much to it, as I have spent ten years in the organization the author has written about. Every word is from the heart and real. Some I have witnessed happening, and others I've heard about since leaving the Singapore operations. Nevertheless, I hold very close to my heart many work values that **MADBiz** has described, for instance MAD @ workplace. We spend a big part of our awake time at work. Thus, it makes so much sense to be working in a workplace that one enjoys to be in. One is lucky if this comes naturally in one's workplace, but in many organizations it doesn't, and the reasons are obvious.

I can testify that the author has taken a lot of effort to transform the organization from a grey nut to one that glows by instilling the four important, simple values. It's not easy, as there were so many obstacles when the author first began to drive change, but the author persevered and had a clear, robust vision. In hindsight, the author, D. Lauren, has great passion, clear vision, and good values, and most importantly, she leads with her heart. She is one of the greatest leaders I have worked with.

Last but not least, "Communicate downward to subordinates with the same care and attention as you communicate upward to superiors." This is the highlight and one precious value that will always stay close to my heart.

This book is more than a worthwhile read; it's a must read!

— H. June,
  Senior Brand Development Manager, Global FMCG Company, China

Having worked under the leadership of D. Lauren for three years, she has taught me many important life's lessons. Today, seven years later, she remains a mentor whose advice I respect, and a lot of her advice is starting to unfold. Despite being a managing director whose plate was super full, she always took time out to coach us, no matter how busy she was. One piece of advice she gave me eventually put me on this path less traveled: being an entrepreneur.

"One never knows how one's life experiences today can help prepare one for the next lap of one's life's journey. Have courage and embrace whatever you have today" was her advice to me. In hindsight, the years I spent working under her became the foundation of what was to come.

In trying times, I remind myself to have courage like D. Lauren. Whatever I learned from her in the past, be it work or life lessons, have already put me in good stead to face whatever I have to overcome. So I don't let myself be the stumbling block. Have courage and charge on, just like her when she believes in something.

I thank her for being the mentor she is to me, and indeed, I am a blessed person for having the good fortune to know her. I will certainly continue to strive on just like her and continue to be MAD for my business. Her advice remains etched in my heart.

I have no doubt **MADBiz** will be a success, for it contains many wise business lessons. It is a must-have for anyone in a corporate job or running a business.

— K. Yan,
Entrepreneur, Personal Care Industry, Singapore

The MAD Culture is an easy and fun-to-read book. It provides many practical examples and hands-on ideas that help ensure impactful delivery on performance. It calls for conscientious effort to shape the results you want to achieve, both in your work and in the marketplace. It encourages the readers to unleash and relish their creativity and potential and daring to be different and aggressive to obtain solutions and enduring results. It is salient for an organization to build team leadership to drive joint responsibility and accountability and to create, orchestrate, and promote high standards of performance to achieve the position of a winning organization. **The MAD Culture** clearly drives this message across.

This book also emphasizes the importance of creating customers' satisfaction through excellent and delightful experiences. I am particularly inspired by D. Lauren's advice: "Delight your customers; engage them not only intellectually but also emotionally, mind to mind and heart to heart. Deliver not just what is required but what is desired!"

In the same breath, the author also imparts the virtues of living and demonstrating good values, having fun at work, and celebrating achievements. This book will inspire you to make a real difference in your workplace and marketplace to achieve extraordinary results!

— L. Jin,
  Senior Banker, Leading Commercial Bank, Australia

The MAD Culture by D. Lauren is a great book for those seeking to make a difference in their work environment. For those who are looking to step up into management or are looking for ways to improve or develop their management skills and/or work ethics, this book will reveal secrets on how to make a difference in all facets of management.

D. Lauren is a go-getter, and she really is an inspiration when it comes to setting goals and getting it done. Her outlook on life and her work ethic are to be commended. She shares stories of her courage at times of fear, and she is certainly someone who continues to inspire me today to do more and to be more.

Most managers remain complacent and wouldn't dare to go the extra mile to identify areas of improvement and therefore limit the potential growth and returns of a company. This book is a must read for those who are ready to make that change and who want to take their careers, relationships, and achievements to a whole new level.

— *Candy White,*
Esolve Business Solutions, Entrepreneur, Personal Care, Beauty and Health Industry, Australia

ISBN: 978-1-4497-4923-1 (e)
ISBN: 978-1-4497-4924-8 (sc)
Library of Congress Control Number: 2012907168

WestBow Press books may be ordered through booksellers or by contacting:

WestBow Press
A Division of Thomas Nelson
1663 Liberty Drive
Bloomington, IN 47403
www.westbowpress.com
1-(866) 928-1240

Printed in the United States of America
WestBow Press rev. date: 5/16/2012

**Making A Difference
in your Business**

The
MAD
Culture

D. Lauren

All my team members and colleagues with whom I've shared some of the greatest moments of life together in making a difference in our workplace and marketplace. Thank you for your unwavering support and trust.

My peers and bosses who have guided me on my learning journey and contributed to my personal development; thank you very much for empowering me to make a difference in my career.

My valued customers, now friends in the marketplace— thank you for giving my team and me the honor to serve and to delight you with memorable experiences. Thank you for giving us the opportunity to make a difference in the marketplace.

All my business partners in the advertising and communication agencies, training consultancies, publishing firms, and other suppliers—thank you for going the extra mile for us. You have made a difference in our businesses.

 *And*

to you who want to

make a difference

in your workplace and marketplace

because
you believe in
leading the change!

Contributor

L. Leo

A creative media professional with a diverse background, Leo received training in photography and audiovisual and video production in the UK and learned film production from the Hollywood pros in the United States in the '90s. More recently, his insatiable appetite for learning led to a master's degree in mass communications from the University of Leicester, followed by recognition from Apple as a certified trainer.

Among the most memorable moments of his thirty-year career as photographer, writer, producer, editor, creative director, and film director were the photographing of President Nelson Mandela for his inaugural election campaign billboard and the shooting of four-by-four adventure documentaries over uncharted terrain in Asia and Africa.

To him, being creative is essentially being different, or to put it the other way around, to be different, you have to be creative. But being creative alone is not enough to triumph in the current business environment; you also need to be at least technically inclined. One of his favorite quotes is, *"All progress occurs because people dare to be different"* (Harry Milner).

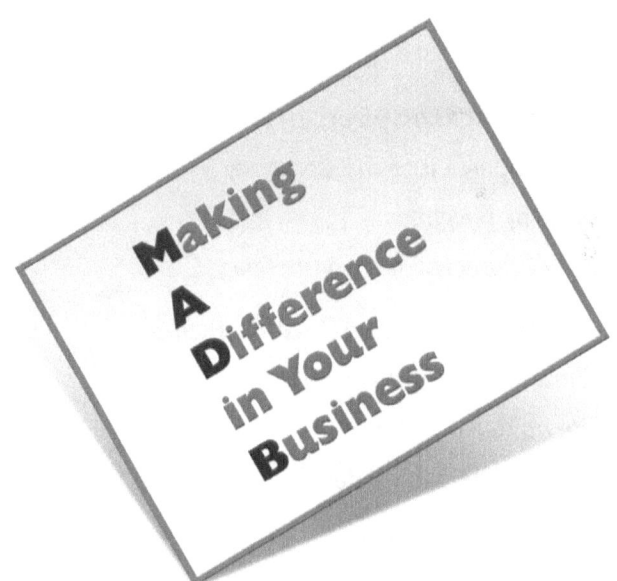

Making A Difference in Your Business

CONTENTS

The MAD Stories

Conclusion

Appendix

MADBiz

is the gateway into the MAD world
of modern business fashioned by the author.

All stories and testimonies quoted in this publication are true;
however, names of the characters have been changed to protect their
identities and as a gesture of respect for their privacy..

PREAMBLE

Making a Difference
in Your Business
during Critical Times!

MADBiz was conceived during a significant time in the recent history of Asia.

The year was 2003. The World Health Organization (WHO) had just announced the outbreak of SARS (Severe Acute Respiratory Syndrome) throughout the continent.

No one was spared—not even the small nation of Singapore. SARS hit Singapore hard, making it one of the worst-hit countries in Asia.

This book describes some principles on organizational culture change and how a work place's transformation can produce high performance of standards which ultimately results in delighting customers. It outlines some innovative practices through several real life management stories and case studies.

What Is Organizational Culture?

Let me briefly outline it this way. An organization is made up of people. They are the ones who shape and deliver the organization's business performance. Their attitudes, behaviors, and approach to work form the characteristics of the organization. In addition, certain patterns, management structures, leadership styles, or traditions/legacies shape the behaviors and perceptions of the people in the organization, and over time, it forms the culture of the organization. Culture is also founded upon shared values, beliefs, assumptions, and expectations, which influence and affect people's way of work and interaction with one another. Culture influences the way things are being done in an organization: *"It's the way we do things here in order to get things done!"*

Hence, before embarking on any business plan or strategy to grow or revive a business, it is essential to put into place the right mindset and heart-set of the people in the organization. Right thinking and actions will transform the climate of the organization and drive the people to perform above par.

In an instant, things changed. Life shifted for many. Travel was restricted, and everyone was asked to check their temperature twice a day as a precaution. Some organizations made it compulsory for their employees to do this, even requiring that temperatures be recorded and submitted to the management daily. In public places everywhere, people began wearing face masks. The media began announcing the number of casualties daily, and while the nation mourned the loss of lives, fear shaded everyday life.

SARS also left many industries reeling. One of the hardest hit was tourism, with impacts on the airline, food and beverage, and hotel industries. Occupancy rates in most hotels fell to a low of 15 percent.

Creating the MAD Culture

MADBiz was conceptualized on the basis that good culture is integral to dynamic growth of an organization and is instrumental in building organizational effectiveness, efficiency, and talents.

MADBiz is an acronym for "making a difference in your business" and focuses on transforming people's behavior to create a healthy and positive organizational culture to deliver the desired results.

Changing a culture is tough enough—it is in the blood of the people—but creating a new culture is like performing blood transfusion many times over! The vision and strategies to transform the organization must be in the organization's DNA. Concerted efforts and initiatives must be taken to incorporate the principles of MADBiz into every business and development plan. To successfully drive the MAD culture, all levels of an organization's hierarchy must be engaged, intellectually and emotionally.

An organization that embraces a MAD Culture will surely produce a positive work climate that encourages and inspires its people to excellence.

Many organizations began adopting across-the-board, harsh belt-tightening measures, from salary cuts to organization-wide restructuring. The cumulative effect of SARS on the economy and the society was fast-becoming a trying and painful lesson for everyone.

While the nation was going through the traumatic experience of SARS, the government and society worked collectively to reduce its spread and impact. From these efforts, one lifechanging idea sprung forth. It was from an individual who stepped away from the atmosphere of fear and uncertainty and embarked on innovative approaches and programs that would eventually change the climate within her own organization and everyone else with whom they came in contact.

Are You MAD?

It is my sincere wish that you will grab hold of the principles of MADBiz to create a MAD culture in your workplace and marketplace and for your personal enrichment. You have to be MAD to create the MAD Culture.

As you read the pages of this book, let your mind be challenged by these questions:

- What type of culture is my organization?
- What type of culture am I developing in my workplace?
- Am I playing an active role to influence or change the culture of my organization?
- Do I have a MAD mind, a MAD attitude, and a MAD spirit?
- Have I been MAD in my work?
- Am I MAD with my customers?
- How can I be more MAD?

And yes! Don't forget to join the the MAD Club. Visit our website for more information at www.madbiz.org.

Let's start our MAD journey!

D. Lauren

are you mad?

INTRODUCTION

Be the One
Who
Makes a Difference!

I have always been an anomaly throughout my career, first as the only rose among the many thorns in the testosterone-infused world of motorsports and then as a reformer and revolutionary in brand marketing.

It is not as if I set out with the conscious ambition to be different. Over time, however, I found that I relished the challenge of being the odd one out. Instead of blending into the background, I chose to position myself at the forefront. And rather than submit to conformity, I gravitated toward diversity. Needless to say, I had to work harder than the rest of my colleagues to prove myself over and over again.

> I found that I relished the challenge of being the odd one out. Instead of blending into the background, I chose to position myself at the forefront.

What ultimately tipped the scales in my favor was that I opted to embrace my uniqueness. In this way, I turned what others perceived as a shortcoming into an advantage. This disposition eventually defined my career. I am proud to state that I made a difference to each and every organization I worked in.

So let's start at the beginning. I cut my teeth in retail marketing at Scott Paper, which is today known as Kimberly

Clark. Later, as the business administrator handling personal care and food service paper products, I worked together with the business manager to spearhead the setting up of the Away-from-Home Division, one of the first in the FMCG (fast-moving consumer goods) industry. My formative years at Scott Paper gave my career a head start and led to my recruitment as the advertising and promotions manager for Silverstone Tyres.

It was at Silverstone that I really came of age. I was one of only a handful of women in the industry and very likely the only one in a senior management position. I stood out like a sore thumb, especially during the motorsports events like Formula Three, 4WD rallies, and overland expeditions involving Silverstone as a sponsor or organizer.

> They gave me a look of utter surprise when I informed them I was the spokesperson for both the sponsor and winning teams!

I cannot recall the number of times I was mistaken for an umbrella girl at the race track! On one occasion, I went to check out a car sprint rally whose organizer was seeking our sponsorship. While I was at the pits, the organizer—who had never met me before—came up and remarked, "Hey, why's there a woman here? This is the wrong place. Umbrella girls outside!" As one of his officers moved to escort me out, I handed the organizer my business card. The look on his face was priceless when he realized his mistake!

Very often during these events, I would be the only female decked out in motorsport attire at the pits, roughing it out with the drivers and crew until the wee hours.

At another international 4WD event where I was managing the Silverstone teams, several journalists were referred to me for comments on an incident. The reporters thought I was there to escort them to the team manager. They gave me a look of utter surprise when I informed them I was the spokesperson for both the sponsor and the winning teams! "Oh, sorry! We didn't expect to see a lady managing 4WD teams!" they said.

Another incident happened during a 4WD expedition to Inner Mongolia. I was part of the advance team to meet the officials of the different provinces in China. Everywhere we went, the local officials were shocked when I was introduced to them as the principal representative of the title sponsor. Many of them had never come across a woman in charge! In one province, they wanted to see what I was made of and challenged me to a few rounds of their local hard liquor. It tasted like kerosene, burning my throat and bringing tears to my eyes. I wouldn't have been surprised to see smoke billowing out from my nose and ears! But I sucked it up, and with the help of team members, we went toe to toe with all of them. By the end of the session, one of the Chinese officials passed out. I could have gone a few more rounds, but fortunately, I didn't have to!

This attitude toward women in power was endemic in the industry. Back home, some of my colleagues would regularly taunt me, although I doubt there was any real malice behind their sarcastic remarks. They would make comments like, "Girl, what do you know about tires? It's only a piece of black rubber to you! Don't waste time! Go back to your tissue job!"

Instead of being intimidated by them, I stood my ground because I was determined to leave my mark in the tire and motorsport industry. I realized I was a pioneer and felt I had the responsibility to change their perception of women in a man's world! During my time at Silverstone Tyres, I found the strength to face each and every challenge and the discipline to endure all the hardship. At times, I had to put on a man's hat to think the way they think, to visualize what was in their minds, and to hear what they did not say. I had to engage them intellectually. But at the same time, I had to balance it with my feminine instincts in preparing and implementing plans.

The strides I made at Silverstone caught others' attention. It was then that I moved on to Unilever Malaysia and later to Unilever Foodservice Singapore. This is the subject of the following chapters.

THE JOURNEY CONTINUES

Going against the Norm

It often requires more courage to dare to do right than to fear to do wrong.
— Abraham Lincoln

It was January 2003. I was sent from my home country to work on the beautiful island of Singapore. It was a dream job; I was appointed the managing director of Unilever (Foodservice), a multinational organization listed on Fortune Global 500.

Needless to say, I was excited at the prospect of spearheading such a prestigious company and the changes that came with it. Not only would I have a new and challenging job, but I would also have new base, a new environment, and new friends and colleagues. Added to that was the prestige of becoming one of the youngest managing directors of this global organization.

These thoughts fueled my enthusiasm, and I set high expectations for myself while eagerly looking forward to meeting these new challenges and achieving new milestones for the company!

In April 2003, everything took a dramatic turn when WHO pronounced Singapore as a severe acute respiratory syndrome (SARS)–hit nation! SARS, which first began in China in November 2002, steadily spread in early 2003, becoming a worldwide pandemic soon afterward. Singapore was not spared.

My company bore the brunt of its impacts, as the hotel segment was our key customer. Morale was affected, and there were growing fears for the physical well-being of every employee and stakeholder. This had a direct effect on the business's operations, and combined with the reduced customer demand for our products and services, there was an overall impact on the levels of business as well. Other industries suffered too. Tourism, entertainment, and the food and beverage industries took a deep dive. Eventually a domino effect created a slump across even unrelated industries. Weariness and a feeling of uncertainty began to grow and grip not merely businesses but also the ordinary citizen. Everyone struggled with the same questions: *How long will this pandemic last? When will the worst be over? When will business pick up again?*

> The last thing you need in a crisis is another crisis!

As in any crisis, solutions can only be found through creative and bold strategies and proactive measures to ensure the growth of the business and the return of normalcy to society. SARS became a painful experience that taught the age-old lessons of resilience in times of trials and tribulations.

Crisis within a Crisis

The last thing you need in a crisis is another crisis!

When I came aboard the new company, I found there was a diffused sense of focus among the various departments. There was little concerted direction and procedure; each head of department was doing things in his or her best but individual way. As a result, the prevailing perception was one of superiority and self-importance, leading to a lack of desire for people to even listen to each other.

This "island" mentality led to a lack of shared goals and empathy between teams. The marketing team did not share the same goals as the sales team. Within the sales team, there was disintegration and dissatisfaction toward channel and customer segmentations. To make matters worse, quite a number of the salespeople did not establish direct contact with their customers, with the exception of chain accounts and some major establishments. There were no customer profiles, and those that existed were rarely updated. Key performance indices (KPI) were not recorded for the sales team; hence, there was no yardstick for achievements or improvements.

The customer service, finance, supply chain, and procurement teams were working independently, with little involvement in the overall business and the strategic and tactical plans. The finance team was also bogged down with a huge number of credit notes due to pricing discrepancies and variations to customers. As a result, it became one of my priorities to settle several backlog credit issues, with some dating back several years to 2000! In addition, I had the regional audit team knocking on my door!

> Every head of department was doing things in their best, but individual ways.

The basic issue, as I saw it, was the poor level of collaboration between departments and even among staff within the same department. It was surely not a conducive workplace for any employee to contribute effectively.

Apart from that, I also noted that the morale of the staff was very low, a rather unsurprising consequence of such a work climate. Another key contributing factor to this low morale was the recent merger of the organization with another large multinational company. Understandably, this precipitated uncertainty and disarray within the management and for the employees of both entities. Hence, my first task was to help the smooth integration of system setup and culture of the two organizations; these included people, structures, systems, products, channels, and customers.

On the Battle Front

On the business front, the market was completely dominated by wholesalers. They were the main channel of distribution for reaching consumers. This channel was critical because it was driving the pattern of the company's monthly sales, and they often dictated the terms and prices of our products! They were tough dealers, demanding very high trade deals or margins for certain fast-moving core products. This in some ways encouraged more parallel imports to enter into the market, and their prices were far more competitive than ours.

The first step to understand the situation was to see what was happening on the ground. I personally conducted market visits, sometimes with and without the sales personnel. To my surprise, I learned that many customers thought that the company had been dissolved and wholesalers were representing us and acting as our agents!

Contact between the company and customers was poor, and I heard comments about customers not having seen our salespeople for many years! The customers also complained about the inconsistent pricing schemes, while wholesalers complained about unfair trade promotions that only benefited the few large businesses that monopolized the market. Worst of all, they said the company did not deliver what it had promised.

Going against the Norm!

I knew I had resort to drastic measures—something that would rock the boat and turn the waves the other way! I knew my decision would not be welcomed, not just by customers, but also by the staff, especially in a time when everyone was dealing with the SARS crisis.

Yet I had little choice, especially because I intended to see the company overcome both the onslaught of the SARS and internal crises. But I did not want them to just survive but to emerge unscathed and triumphant!

I knew that under such tough circumstances, even if I had the

perseverance of strong management of and steadfast commitment to the people, these attributes would still not be sufficient to achieve the kind of results we wanted. What was needed was something different, something out of the norm, something aggressive and bold to be initiated and implemented both in the workplace and in the marketplace. And it had to be done really fast as well!

> But I did not want them to just survive, but to emerge, unscathed and triumphant!

The Birth of

MADBIZ

A Fresh Approach

It was July 2003. The World Health Organization finally gave a clean bill of health to Singapore. With it came the lifting of all advisories against travel to the country.

However, the collective effects of SARS and the toll it had exacted on the economy and the people proved to be too severe. Still, the announcement came as a relief to many. The worst nightmare was finally over!

But I was about to witness and experience the beginning of another crisis. I had anticipated it and was prepared to face it. This crisis would propel the business to greater heights. How was that possible? The answer was simple; it was all about making and delivering the difference to achieve our desired results.

The significant problems we face cannot be solved at the same level of thinking we were at when we created them.

— Albert Einstein

Battling the Odds

Post-SARS, July 2003.

Wholesalers cry foul over new distributorship system and pricing structure!

Revamping of business structure! Salespeople resign en bloc!

Three major bypasses! Will the sick patient survive?

Unthinkable! It's MAD!

These were some of the headlines and sentiments expressed by staff and the wholesalers when I announced the plan and immediate implementation of three major exercises!

These three major exercises covered the setting up of a distributorship and logistics system, price restructuring and introduction of wholesalers' incentives, and streamlining of sales teams to ensure good coverage of all our customers.

However, in response to the implementation of these major exercises, many salespeople resigned en bloc. There were various reasons for their collective action; some may have done it to protest the business decisions while a few were not confident they could fulfill the new standards of assessment. The rest who remained had reservations about the success of my plans.

As anticipated, the wholesalers who were not selected to be distributors and whose margins were reduced drastically were very upset. They resorted to shouting, scolding,

cursing, and hurling criticism during our sales calls. They even threatened to stop buying from the company, demanding that, if they continued, they should enjoy the same margins.

As was expected, competitors took advantage of this market hostility toward the company during this difficult period. Seizing the opportunity, they set out to worsen our relationship with wholesalers by offering increased support in terms of incentives and free goods.

Risky, Unorthodox Approach!

There is no doubt that the plan I implemented was risky and unorthodox, particularly from the aspect of its timing and execution. Since the beginning, the organization had depended completely on wholesalers to sell our products to commercial customers; now, however, we were sending our own sales team directly to these customers. This new practice was viewed as a threat to undermine the wholesalers' business. Moreover, this was done immediately after the SARS pandemic while many businesses were still depressed and had not gotten back on their feet again.

> Business is all about strategy, timing and execution; the right strategy; the right timing; the right execution.

However, business is all about strategy, timing, and execution—the right strategy, the right timing, and the right execution. These were, in my opinion, the deciding factors that determined the success of great plans. While many plans and ideas are great, they fail because of wrong timing and poor execution. While goals and strategies are easy to formulate, success hinges on effective implementation or execution.

Many failures have their roots in poor execution. The real skills lie in executing the plans and strategies well.

I was asked this question by many of my acquaintances: "*What was the basis for implementing the drastic measures, especially at a time when your staff and key customers' businesses had yet to recover from the effects of the SARS pandemic?*"

Drivers have to look out for danger spots, hair-pin curves and jumps that leave the car vulnerable to going off course.

This is a good question indeed. This was my reply: I know there are many schools of thought on how best to handle integrations and business restructuring, especially during crisis times, which in our case was during the SARS pandemic. I heard murmurs coming even from top management, but I refused to allow them to affect me. I knew exactly what I was embarking on. I already knew the kind of results I was working to achieve. I chose not to flow along with the fear and uncertainties that were clouding the atmosphere. Instead, I was shaping the plans and strategies to achieve these desired results.

During those trying times, I drew on my past career experiences. I saw myself like a rally driver who had to steer through a hostile market environment and the competition's activities while overcoming internal conflicts. During a rally, the driver has to take charge of his vehicle and set his sights on completing the race. Rally cars do not just race on a fixed and paved course. Instead, rallies take place in a natural environment on a course that may include any and every type of ground conditions imaginable. Drivers have to look out for danger spots, hair-pin curves, and jumps that leave the car vulnerable to going off course. It is not only a race against time, but it is also a race against the endurance of the machine and our physical body, mind, and emotions. The driver and navigator must be equipped to handle any eventualities where extreme endurance and driving techniques are tested to get around the course competitively.

It is very much a similar scenario in the marketplace. I had to adopt the same strategic moves—the right strategies, the right execution, and the right timing.

> I knew I had to quickly lay a solid, workable foundation upon which to build. If I were to transform the future of the business by drastically changing the way or the system on which the business had been operating for decades, so be it.

When I was about to embark on this plan, one of my senior managers asked me a question. While some people may have acted with more caution, I felt that it boosted my confidence and emboldened me further to move ahead with my plans.

He asked me, *"You are conducting three major bypasses on a patient; this patient has been sick for some time and has not been responding to attempts at recovery. Can you be very sure that this sick patient will survive these major operations?"*

To this question, I confidently replied yes, because I already saw opportunities in this "sick patient." I remembered the words of Winston Churchill: "A pessimist sees the difficulty in every opportunity; an optimist sees the opportunity in every difficulty."

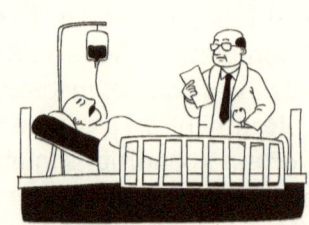

I knew I had to embark on this surgery because the time was right (the arteries had been blocked far too long!), although it would require a lot from everyone to see its success. I knew I had to quickly lay a solid, workable foundation upon which to build. If I were to transform the future of the business by drastically changing the way or the system on which the business had been operating for decades, so be it.

> ... nurturing a culture of loving the customers and people in an organization.

Throughout years of experience, I have seen many innovative products that were knocked off the shelves simply because they were not firmly supported by a competent and robust system. Many organizations have overlooked the fact that it will be much harder for competitors to eliminate or replicate their business system than your products when their system is locked or weaved into an integrated chain of management where each supports the other's function, particularly when this is founded on solid management leadership. Products can be easily copied and improved upon—but not a robust business system!

You may ask me, "What is your interpretation of an innovative and robust business system?"

Let me answer in these words. It is a business that comes with a well-integrated manufacturing, sales and marketing, customer support, and logistics system to enable the production of a continuing stream of attractive, innovative product that will meet your targeted markets' needs and desires while nurturing a culture of loving the customers and people in an organization. This involves cultivating excellent customer management with a superb level of response to their needs and close, direct contacts with the distribution channel and customers. Of immense importance is that every staff member feels valuable and is a significant contributor to the growth of the organization.

> **Of immense importance is that every staff member feels valuable and is a significant contributor to the growth of the organization.**

Obviously, this is easier said than done! But I had decided, and I continued to press on and press ahead. I was steadfast despite massive objections and expressions of frustration and disappointment from many people.

During this tumultuous period, I put into practice some of the lessons that I had learned in my previous jobs. I remembered a nugget of wisdom that a former boss had shared with me: "*Being at the top is not all beautiful. It has roses, but they are surrounded by thorns. Often it is lonely up there! You may make tough decisions that people won't like you for. They can't see the roses in your decisions but only the thorns prickling them. But you must be able to see both the roses and thorns!*"

I found this to be true. Many of my staff seemed to distance themselves from me. They seemed to be avoiding contact. While they appeared eager to see my next move in countering the objections from the market, I sensed that they came into meetings with a feeling of doom and gloom.

Through instituting the three major exercises together, I also made a decision to bleed once instead of thrice. What I mean is that it was better to let the market get really upset with the company once during the economic slowdown than on three separate occasions when businesses had recovered. I envisaged the impact would be worse and greater during the latter phase of recovery. I decided to let the volcano erupt once and experience the pain, immense as it would be, all at once!

Once we had set up the right business system, comprising structure and foundation, we shifted all our energies into mending relationships and growing the business. I was confident that the new team would do a better and speedier job to reconcile these disgruntled wholesalers. At the same time, we also established strong contacts and direct touch points with the commercial customers in order to strengthen our position in the marketplace as a preferred business partner. Once we as a company were favored by our customers, wholesalers could then be persuaded to adopt a different attitude toward us. I had planned everything carefully. Ultimately I wanted to assure both wholesalers and commercial customers that we had integrity and they could partner with us with confidence for better growth.

> I also made a decision to bleed once instead of thrice.

During the entire process of integration and re-structuring, I would be lying if I said that I did not experience any anxiety at all. The entire burden of accountability was placed on my shoulders, and I constantly thought of the scenario should the plan not work the way I hoped. In my mind, there was a long

list of what ifs. For example, I would think, *What if more and more staff resigns? What if every wholesaler sabotages us despite our endeavor to keep their loyalty? What if the new sales team is not ready or is unable to face the battle and leaves? What if the appointed distributors fail to deliver their tasks? What if …?* However, as a leader, I could not divulge my anxieties to the team because they had their own humiliations with the customers to deal with.

I knew I needed to be calm and strong, stay focused on results rather than obstacles, and continue to be passionate to encourage and motivate them to look forward. They needed to stay focused, persevere, be strong, and delight the customers because I believed that we were already on the right track to achieving success!

At this juncture, I recalled a similar situation at Silverstone Tyres. The event was an overland 4WD expedition from Malaysia to Inner Mongolia that would span thirty-two days and eighteen thousand kilometers. It was a record-breaking expedition and a true test to the endurance of man and machine over the tough terrain across four nations.

While the convoy was driving through the hairpin turns of the mountainous province of Yunnan in China, one of the vehicles skidded and fell into a deep ravine. It was late at night, and no one knew the vehicle was lost until they had reached the campsite. It was a small town. The local police were called in to search for the lost vehicle. However, they were unable to offer

> **I knew that I needed to be calm and strong, stay focused on results rather than obstacles, and continue to be passionate.**

much help because it was too dark for them to conduct the search. At that time, I was not part of the convoy because I was still in Malaysia. I was scheduled to meet them later in Beijing. That particular vehicle was carrying a journalist from a leading national daily and another two crew members who were experienced off-roaders who had clinched several 4WD competition championships!

When I received the news, I was obviously deeply concerned and anxious over the safety of the vehicle members. But how was I going to break the news to the chief editor of the newspaper? How was I going to explain that we had no information on their whereabouts and whether they were safe or not? I was in an extremely stressful and difficult position. The editors kept calling to get an update on the situation, but I didn't have much information to go by. I could only wait by the phone and hope for the best. At one stage, I couldn't think straight. My anxiety kept mounting. But I knew I had to stay calm and strong! I could not afford to panic because this would in turn cause more alarm. I had to straighten my head and focus on getting the important and urgent things done right and straight away.

> **Anything that can go wrong, will go wrong.**

Eventually, the vehicle was found. It was saved by several big trees in the ravine! It was hanging by the trees some three hundred meters down the ravine. The vehicle was badly damaged, but the three passengers inside the vehicle escaped unhurt. It was a miracle, but the whole ordeal was a terrifying nightmare for everyone! By then I had the press release prepared, and I had all the necessary spare parts for the damaged modified vehicle packed and off. I then boarded the next flight to Kunming, the capital of Yunnan.

The expedition had to continue. We could not allow the accident to derail the focus, purpose, objective, and goal of the expedition. Such experiences taught me to handle and manage crises objectively and confidently. It also prepared me to be ready when Murphy's Law strikes, especially when you least expect it to. Anything that can go wrong will go wrong.

Now, with the current crisis in at Unilever, I had to renew my mind with positive thoughts and align my perspective to focus on the purpose and objective of the whole exercise. I had to apply the same fortitude I had acquired in my past experiences.

To overcome all these mind-boggling questions and constant mental bombardments, I kept to the course of action, staying proactive and quick with tactical planning. I would always try to anticipate how the market might react or retaliate. I had to be ever ready, arming my team and myself with solutions whenever the salespeople sounded the alarm. We had to be there anytime and anywhere for our people and customers whenever they needed us.

> We had to be there, anytime and anywhere for our people and customers whenever they needed us.

With the en masse resignation of the sales team, a decision was made to hire fresh graduates to form the new sales team. To ensure this new team was imbued with the right qualities from the start, I engaged a very experienced sales manager who had an excellent track record in coaching and selling. The new sales staff was immediately immersed with relevant sales competencies, product knowledge, and applications and KPIs.

Along with the new sales team, several new staff members were recruited to manage the customer service and marketing functions. An important part of their core duties was to conduct regular market visits to encourage better understanding of the business, gain customers' insights, and provide constructive feedback to the sales team. They had to sit with the sales team in most meetings to align their perspectives and ensure their emotional engagement with all sales activities. In addition, they were roped into sales training so they would have an in-depth understanding of sales competencies and expectations, customers' behavior, and sales objections. The hiring of a new team for both sales and marketing was not welcomed by many, who saw this as being ridiculous and foolish, particularly in the light of such a critical period for the economy.

> **Establishing a strong mentoring and coaching system was another way of helping the sales team face and overcome their fears and disappointments.**

To keep the staff motivated and inspired, I would create an atmosphere that made them feel happy and excited about coming to work each day. It was important to make them proud of being part of the organization despite the prevailing circumstances. We rolled out the company's core values, which were being passionate, caring, sharing, and courageous. These were accompanied by many activities, which everyone was encouraged to practice daily. Eventually these values became a way of life within the organization.

Establishing a strong mentoring and coaching system was another way of helping the sales team face and overcome their fears and disappointments. This also encouraged them to stay focused and keep moving forward.

Soon, a new work climate was created; a healthy, positive culture was established. It cushioned the hard market impacts that the team were facing and boosted their morale. They were now united and extending support to each other every day. Together, these integrated efforts accelerated their learning curve dramatically.

Winning the Hearts of the industry

While I was busy tackling and managing the wholesalers' and internal staff crises, I did not forget the commercial customers—hotels, restaurants, fast food chains, local eateries, bakeries, hospitals, and the education segment. This segment of customers played a very crucial role in growing the organization's business. While the wholesalers were integral to the distribution side of the business, the commercial customers were our end-users. The chefs, the F&B managers, the purchasers, and the housekeeping managers were decision makers of the type of products and brands to be consumed in their outlets. We needed their support to grow our business. Otherwise, the business would be relying heavily on the distribution channel for sales and growth, which was not healthy business wise.

The food and beverage industry was still reeling from the effects of SARS. Our business relationships with commercial customers were not strong due to past strategies and poor management of customers. We had to break off and erase the poor perceptions they had of us if we wanted to break through. While the sales manager was busy equipping the new sales team, I engaged the help of a professional video production house to feature a story on the Singapore food and beverage industry. In the documentary, we paid tribute to their role and contribution to the country's wealth; F&B was a main driver of the nation's economy. We interviewed several movers and shakers of the industry, who gave some insights into the practices of the industry, issues and challenges the industry was facing, and the impact of SARS on their businesses. We showed that in the face of great adversity, the F&B community displayed even greater resilience. Their determined spirit had overcome all obstacles and emerged stronger than ever.

> **We mend the 'bridge over troubled waters'; we continued to work hard to strengthen the bridge and fastened it.**

We highlighted their commitment and efforts to establish the nation's culinary prowess in the international scene, putting Singapore on the international culinary map and making it the food paradise it is today. The video also served as a platform for the industry to create public awareness of the collective efforts of the many dedicated and passionate F&B professionals and bodies that had made Singapore recognized as a world-class F&B hub. These video documentaries were distributed free to all F&B institutions, culinary schools, associations, media owners, and F&B events and trade exhibitions.

This initiative was very well received by the industry. It was a morale booster for them, especially after the SARS onslaught. It was a highly valued recognition that the industry had not had. They appreciated our effort to show support for them in times of trials. This was the first initiative we took to gain back the confidence, trust, and respect from the commercial customers for our organization. From there, we mend the "bridge over troubled waters"; we continued to work hard to strengthen the bridge and fastened it.

Knowing that such tributes were important to inspire the industry to greater heights, we continued doing them but in different forms for the following two years. It was also our sincere way of thanking them for their renewed support in us. Without their support, we wouldn't be there! It was a win-win partnership!

Every staff was involved in the business! Every staff was required to know his or her customers!

Results!

It was December 2003. After five months of persistent door-knocking and courageously facing the customers with passion and humility, the teams' efforts paid off handsomely. We cocooned customers in many ways, always offering solutions that worked in their best interests. We were proactive and offered creative ideas to grow their businesses. Not only were the customers being called on by the sales teams, but the marketing and customer service team called on them as well and readily provided them with marketing support materials and programs. If there was any dispute in credit control and accounts receivables, the finance personnel would also pay a visit to the customer to settle the dispute immediately. Every staff member was involved in the business! Every staff member was required to know his or her customers.

From the sales force to the back-room staff, every individual earned not only praise but also respect from the customers. We also saw a high success rate in customers' returning preference for the company's products as well as a significant increase in new accounts and penetration of products.

Apart from this, the company abolished pricing discrepancies among wholesalers. With consistent pricing policies and a fair trade deal structure, the once-disgruntled wholesalers began to welcome the sales team. Customers soon discovered that we were serious and passionate about doing business with them, displaying a genuine interest in seeing their business prosper. We proved that we possessed integrity.

> Customers soon discovered that we were serious and passionate about doing business with them, displaying a genuine interest in seeing their business prosper. We proved that we possessed integrity.

In tandem with our better customer relationships, account receivables improved by a whopping 50 percent! We also had access to updated customers' database and sales performance, which helped us to analyze, identify, and take the necessary actions to boost sales productivity.

All these led to a turnaround in the company, with a positive change in customer perception. We were now regarded as an organization that was committed to deliver.

It was a team effort, with team leadership playing its role effectively. Every staff member was diligent and contributed accordingly. Everyone displayed a sense of ownership. Every individual was important to the company. The core values were successfully incorporated into their work culture and became part of their everyday behavior and a way of life.

> Their passion to achieve results shaped their attitude and enlarged their capacity to reach beyond what they could not reach or feared before.

The renewed energy, passion, and courage also drove the team to achieve what was impossible before. Their conviction and belief in the values of the company and the leadership impacted the way they behaved. Their passion to achieve results shaped their attitude and enlarged their capacity to reach beyond what they could not reach or feared before. It inspired them and opened their hearts and minds to change. They began to learn and understand the business faster than ever.

More importantly, they began to understand the meaning of respect, trust, and integrity. Relationships improved when interpersonal sensitivity grew and made a difference, not only in the workplace but also in the marketplace. Every success was celebrated, and soon customers called us *"the best team in town!"* This was how we became a truly winning team!

Business Results

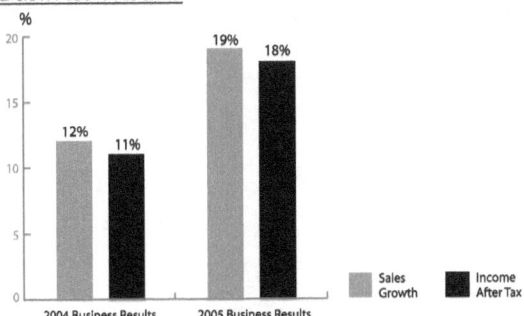

Global People Survey 2004 –
Top in Leadership, People Organization,
Organization Culture & Climate.

President's Award for Outstanding Achievements for :

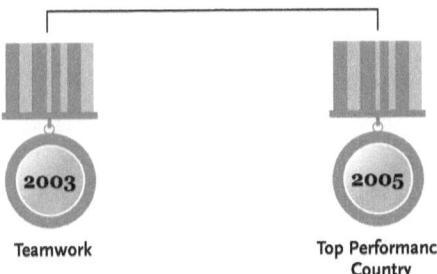

2003
Teamwork

2005
Top Performance
Country

Sales Team Awarded:

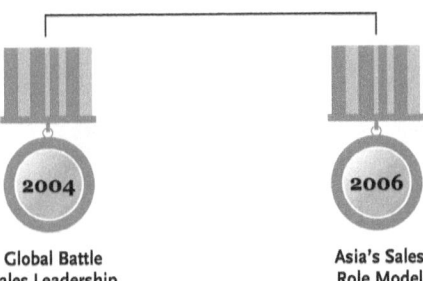

2004
Global Battle
Sales Leadership

2006
Asia's Sales
Role Model

are you mad?

The Three
BUILDING BLOCKS of

Creating the MAD Culture

The biggest return on investment
comes from investing in employees.
Employees are always more important
than the company,
its assets, and its stock.

— Paul J. Meyer

The First Building Block …

Inspired

@

Workplace

Great men are little men expanded;
great lives are ordinary lives intensified.
— Wilfred A. Peterson

1

I Am Important to the Company!

The staff members are important and contributing stake-owners of an organization.

An organization is made up of people. Without people, there are no organizations. People must be seen as the number-one asset. We must recognize that everyone wants to feel important and to contribute. When an organization recognizes the value of its people and treats them as stake-owners, everyone will benefit.

It is the management's role to instill a sense of ownership and belonging in every member of the staff by:

- Making an effort to agree to and align clear expectations and goals with all staff

- Delegating and empowering not only leaders but also every level of staff. This includes allowing staff to make decisions, take actions, lead, and create shared or collective responsibility to achieve results. When empowering them, both sides must agree on the scope, budget, resources, expected deliverables, and timeframe of the job. Empowerment means that trust must exist on both sides.

Besides these, the management plays a key role in:

- Observing, monitoring, and reviewing progress to ensure delivery of results. They must be in the loop to offer support, assistance, and advice while being involved in the substance and final details of the key execution, strategic directions and operations, and the growth of leadership and staff personal development;

- Engaging, shaping, and coaching team leaders in their responsibilities to drive leadership commitment, accountability, and performance. Every established leader should work toward producing and building more leaders, and not more followers.

- Directing the staff to perceive things from "the top" or a wider perspective. This would involve cascading the vision, expectations, plans, and performance progress to all levels of staff on a quarterly basis. Such actions enable the staff to have greater clarity and alignment with the mission of the organization.

> Give to us clear vision that we may know
> where to stand and what to stand for—
> because unless we stand for something
> we shall fall for anything.
> — Peter Marshall

- Constantly communicating with staff to define, align, and reinforce growth plans to ensure that every staff member understands and is motivated to support and deliver growth. Good communication enhances confidence and trust.

Communicate downward to subordinates
with at least the same care and attention
as you communicate upward to superiors.
— L. B. Belker

- Inspiring the staff to commit to the vision by engaging their hearts and minds and connecting with them in ways that give sense to their inspirations and hopes. Communicate passionately about your values, convictions, beliefs, and hopes, and put them into daily practice. Speak to them on a personal level because people will internalize your vision and message and make it theirs when they are connected to you. Be the living example for them to look up to; this will give them good reasons to follow your lead.

A leader is a dealer in hope.
— Napoleon Bonaparte

- Building commitment in the team. Without commitment, it will be impossible to realize your vision. Commitment grows when people have faith in you and will even sail with you through storms. Such faith springs from constant communication and the examples you set through your actions. Do not ask people to do anything that you would not do. They will judge your words and deeds as a measure of your own commitment to the vision.

- Engage every staff member in the vision for growth and plans of the organization in order to get their "buy-in." Encourage their active and aggressive participation and contributions. There should be no spectators; everyone is a participant and a contributor to success.

Walk the Talk!

This is not armchair management! Move around and know your people. Be accessible to your staff. Be a people person if you want them to support and fulfill your vision, for if you want them to serve your goals and dreams, you must first serve their needs. Today's leader is here to serve. Then and only then will you be served. Accordingly, be the first to honor. Then you will also be honored.

> The first responsibility of a leader is to define reality.
> The last is to say thank you.
> In between the leader is a servant.
> — Max DePree

 ## Be a Good Listener

Keep your ears to the ground. Listen to people, especially those in the front line who talk to customers. When management shows a genuine interest in their views and advice, the staff will feel appreciated and important. Remember, everyone wants to be heard.

> Think like a wise man but communicate
> in the language of the people.
> — William Yeats

Encourage an Environment of Democratic Involvement

Democracy is based upon the conviction
that there are extraordinary possibilities
in ordinary people.
— Harry Emerson Fosdick

- Do not fear instilling a free flow of discussion or views. Do not discourage or penalize those who voice their disagreements to your views. Be calm and objective; focus on receiving constructive criticism. Make constructive criticism work for the benefit of the organization. Do not be defensive.

Criticism may not be agreeable, but it is necessary.
It fulfills the same function as pain in the human body:
It calls attention to an unhealthy state of things.
— Sir Winston Churchill

- Cultivate openness in sharing ideas, and involve every staff member in generating ideas at meetings or workshops. Wherever possible, incorporate their ideas as ways of improving the business.

The best way to have a good idea
is to have lots of ideas.
— Linus Pauling

- Every idea must be received with an open mind and a positive spirit. Your staff will only feel comfortable expressing their ideas and opinions when they know the management is receptive and appreciative and genuinely values their opinions in pursuing positive change and growth.

- The most creative and best ideas or solutions are normally conceived by people when they are challenged or when they feel most relaxed and not fearful about unleashing their imagination and creativity.

- When people are inspired by an organization's visions and believe that they are important assets in their workplace because their welfare and progress are well taken care of, the results are positive.

- The staff will not focus on thoughts such as, "What are my benefits?" but are more likely to think, "What and how can I contribute to grow *my* company?"

- They will take more pride in and assume ownership of their work.

- They will take the initiative and timely, proactive measures to deliver what the organization demands of them.

- They will be passionate about their jobs, care about their competencies, and desirous of improvement as proof of their ability, especially to those who are looking at their performance!

Recognize Good Work, and Celebrate Achievements!

Every human being needs reassurance of his abilities and values. Everyone appreciates receiving compliments when he or she performs well. Recognition and praise are the best ways to inspire people!

- Use sincere words of praise when they are warranted. Words are free but worth a fortune when they are well chosen and spoken in a timely way.

- Celebrating achievements is not an act of flattery or for ego-boosting. It is a thoughtful and heartwarming way of recognizing and rewarding excellent efforts and outstanding performances.

- Promote and endorse good performance and enhance the reputation of those who have contributed to growth. People give you their best when they know they will be rewarded and recognized for excellent character and work.

- Develop a creative program that rewards high achievers and those who conscientiously display and work toward creating a better environment and work culture.

- Show gratitude to your staff, and they will scale the mountains for you!

> Next to ingratitude the most painful thing
> to bear is gratitude.
> — Henry Ward Beecher

I alone can do a few things;
but together,
we can do a lot of big things!

— Mother Theresa

Love Thy Neighbor

Examine the prevailing climate of your organization, in particular the working conditions and atmosphere and the behavior of the staff. Understand the underlying issues affecting their behavioral patterns, and identify ways of correcting or further improving them without having to demean the existing circumstances.

• Bring on the right climate! It must be one that drives positive results by introducing and building some core values in people. Observe, evaluate, and ascertain which core values are critical and integral to the achievement of your vision. These values can be defined as being caring, compassionate, courageous, committed, humble, passionate, respectful, responsible, trustworthy, sharing, serving, etc. The selected core values must become part of their daily habits and practices. It requires conscious effort in the beginning to practice these values, but over time, they may become a natural part of one's personality and behavior. They will live in and through those who practice them, and the result will be a healthier and more positive work climate.

• A caring and sharing culture will encourage people to be honest about their mistakes and shortcomings even as it gives them the confidence to seek ways to correct them. In a negative climate, people tend to complain, cover up their mistakes, or deny their errors. They may even blame others and create the impression that they are victims. In a less caring environment, negative emotions such as hostility, resentment, insecurity, anger, and jealousy will prevail. Such must be prevented at all costs.

Kind words can be short and easy to speak, but their echoes are truly endless.
— Mother Teresa

Leaders must show the way in living these core values daily, first by embracing them and acting them out daily. This is leading by example. This top-down style is necessary. Otherwise leaders will be regarded as hypocrites who mouth words without actions. This will result in loss of integrity and respect.

• Leaders must create an atmosphere of integrity, accountability, respect, and stability in order to build a strong, healthy, and successful team. This will prevent slandering, strife, misplaced criticism, gossip, and irresponsibility between people.

The spirit of an organization is created from the top.
— Peter Drucker

• If you want people to do things that they are unable to do now, you must provide support by gently pushing their horizons. Coach them to break their self-imposed limitations and encourage confidence to grow so they can over-reach themselves to accomplish things they never thought were possible. Create conditions for improvement and excellence so they can utilize their skills and talents to achieve their own and the organization's goals. This is in line with promoting a coaching culture.

- Promote team commitment. Forge team leadership. Strengthen the spirit of camaraderie. Encouraging cohesiveness and team spirit are essential ingredients to achieving maximum results. It is said that teamwork divides the task but doubles the success rate.

> I hear and I forget.
> I see and I remember.
> I do and I understand.
> — Chinese Proverb

Do Unto Others as You Want Others to Do Unto You

- This is a familiar wise saying that is not easy to emulate. Why? Because everyone wants to be right, liked, and treated well. However, not everyone has the initiative or the willingness to take the first step in treating others the way they would like to be treated.

- Remember, everything starts with a first step. Without this, there is no journey to savor. If everyone waits for someone to make the first move, nobody will start. Nothing will happen because everyone will wait for everyone else. In the words of St. Augustine, "There is no greater invitation to love than loving first."

> **They do not love that**
> **do not show their love.**
> **— William Shakespeare**

- We often refuse to initiate kind gestures because of past negative experiences or simply because we dislike certain characters. Keep in mind that in everyone's life, there is something hidden deep within that has had an impact or influences the way we carry ourselves. Nobody likes to make mistakes, and nobody likes to be disliked by others. When your colleague makes a mistake, do not make a scene. When you are offended, learn to forgive. When your colleague acts in a certain manner that does not go down well with you, be understanding. Remind yourself that you do not know what happened to your colleague before he or she left home that morning. Extend your hand of understanding to your teammates. Help your teammates succeed.

- However, we must not endorse bad characters, for they are like malignant cancerous cells: they grow and spread if not discovered early enough. When you do discover them, have them removed.

> **My words fly up, my thoughts remain below;**
> **Words without thoughts**
> **Never to heaven go.**
> **— William Shakespeare**

- It is essential that everyone in an organization learn to accept one another and enjoy working with one another as a family. We cannot deny that is not easy to love all people. It is easy to love those who love you; however, to love someone who is unlovable or who speaks unkindly of you is probably the hardest thing. Still, we can at least try our best to show kindness and respect to everyone around us.

The best and most beautiful things
in life cannot be seen, not touched,
but are felt in the heart.
— Helen Keller

Create Fun @ Work!

Create a friendly family atmosphere where strong bonding exists among colleagues and between management. Do not create a stressful workplace where the management or team leaders impose unreasonable practices, discipline, pressures, or deadlines on the staff. There must be a good balance of all aspects to achieve maximum productivity.

• A good working climate inspires productivity because the staff members love and enjoy what they are doing. The workplace must be shaped in such a way that the staff can look forward to coming in daily because they feel wanted and cared for. It must be a place where they know they can be their best because it is built on good, solid values. It is not just about working but loving what they do for a living. Their jobs have become their passion! It must be a place they enjoy and where they find satisfaction and fulfillment. They will not consider quitting even when the going gets tougher and tougher because they love what they are doing and are committed to seeing strong, positive results.

When we accept tough jobs as a
challenge and wade into them with
joy and enthusiasm,
miracles can happen.
— Gilbert Arland

- An unhappy staff member can be recognized easily by his productivity. An unhappy person is not productive simply because he is no longer passionate about his work. Often, he will not be able to fulfill the expectations of the organization not because he is incapable or lacks competency, but rather because he is disillusioned, dissatisfied, or unfulfilled. When a person is not passionate or excited about his work, it shows in his attitude, behavior, and output. Carelessness and mistakes will occur frequently because these are the results of a person who lacks enthusiasm in his work.

- Encourage an atmosphere of learning and expanding work horizons and contributions. Be willing to invest time and effort to develop personal growth. When the staff members know that the organization believes in training and developing them, they will naturally re-invest what they have learned into the organization.

Learning is acquired by reading books,
but the much more necessary learning,
the knowledge of the world,
is only to be acquired by
reading men and studying all
the various facets of them.
— Lord Chesterfield

- Lighten up the workplace by making the atmosphere fun and warm. Put up heartwarming and creative decorations during festive seasons, or set a theme or slogan to reinforce the vision or core values of the organization. The workplace must be comfortable and relaxing for the mind and body. Also, make it exciting and fun. Let energy and creativity flow freely in your workplace. Your workplace is your second home (to some, it may be the first home!); hence, you deserve an upbeat environment that brings out the best in you.

- A fun and exciting workplace will brighten the mood of the people working in it. A good mood makes for better work, higher productivity, and greater successes.

**A person who lives to age seventy-five
has 657,000 hours of life.
This is too long a period not to have fun!**

A man of character
will make himself worthy
of any position he is given.

— Mahatma Gandhi

3

Build Character and Competence—C & C

Create a climate that inspires positive change and growth through words, actions, priorities, and performance.

- Every piece of work you do and every word you say is a self-portrait or reflection of yourself.

- Our outlook is basically influenced by what we believe of ourselves and how we think others see us. This eventually determines our output, be it our behavior, our character, our actions, our performance, our credibility, etc. Our output will eventually shape our destiny.

- Therefore, it is the role and responsibility of every organization to effectively instill and shape their staff to think, believe, and live positively so that they can deliver results based on their fullest potential and capability.

> Treat people as if they were what they ought to be
> and you help them to become
> what they are capable of being.
> — Johann Wolfgang Von Goethe

Cultivate a positive mental attitude (PMA) approach in your organization by imparting knowledge and development training to staff, developing a positive mindset through consciously living some key core values, instilling an active learning culture, and building inspiring team leadership.

- Bring the staff to the level of understanding, appreciating and actualizing the real meaning of having and operating in a PMA. Without a clear understanding of how to engage in a PMA and the benefits of doing so, the strategy will not work because staff members will lack the belief in what is good and beneficial for them. When there is no conviction or belief, your efforts will be fruitless.

- When an organization operates under the climate of a PMA, the mindset will view negative situations as challenges for improvements and seek for positive ways and means to offset negativities. Someone with a PMA will not look at negative situations negatively; instead, he or she will engage in the right and proper perspective and work toward maximizing the situation to the benefit of the organization. In short, he or she will turn negatives into positives!

- A PMA is receptive and can originate new, innovative ideas, concepts, and solutions while believing in the impossible. The mind is not closed and fixed but instead has the ability to stretch, receive, and process new paradigms that are not viewed as viable by others who operate within the normal mental paradigm.

That's what learning is, after all:
not whether we lose the game, but how we lose
and how we've changed because of it,
and what we take away from it that we never had before,
to apply to other games.
Losing, in a curious way, is winning.
— Richard Bach

- A person with a PMA has a resourceful mind. He or she will think outside the box and move beyond boundaries to find solutions. He or she has the capacity to seek alternative plans, directions, or solutions that will best overcome a situation and produce the desired results.

> Most people are more satisfied with
> old problems than committed
> to finding new solutions.
> — John Maxwell

- Therefore, instill and consciously drive the core values that you have introduced to challenge others' mental attitudes, as this can change the behavior and outer aspects of their lives.

> We are what we repeatedly do.
> Excellence, then, is not an act,
> but a habit.
> — Aristotle

Evaluate conduct, including aspects of discipline, performance, and integrity via a multisource 360-degree feedback.

- This feedback should come from different staff levels from different departments or divisions that have dealings with them on a regular basis. The source of such feedback should be kept anonymous to prevent bad feelings. Multisource feedback will encourage all staff to engage in fair conduct and be consistent with all colleagues, regardless of seniority.

- This method of providing the leadership with constructive feedback is aimed at instituting improvements without de-motivating others or affecting their self-esteem. Whenever there are positive comments, leaders must communicate these to the staff concerned, as well as show some form of appreciation while encouraging and inspiring them to further excel.

- Do not compromise on quality of work and character, particularly from the aspect of discipline.

> **It isn't the incompetent who destroy an organization.**
> **The incompetent never get in a position to destroy it.**
> **It is those who have achieved something and**
> **want to rest upon their achievements**
> **who are forever clogging things up.**
> **— F. M. Young**

Get the Right Person for the Job

Do not be tempted to hire the best person in town for a particular job. Hire the right person instead—someone who is able to adapt to and adopt the organization's visions, goals, and culture of work. In this respect, the best person in town is not always the right person. Even though his educational background and work experience may qualify him for the position, he may not be suited to hold the responsibilities of the position because he cannot fit into the organization's culture and work environment.

- Do not attempt to place an individual in a position of responsibility for which he is not prepared, equipped, or suited. This is placing him in the wrong task or in a position that proves his incompetence. This is sometimes true even though the change is a lateral move within the organization. Regardless of how good the staff member was in his previous position, he may sometimes be unable to deliver the same level of effectiveness and efficiency when he is placed in the wrong position. Eventually he ends up frustrated, overworked, and underproductive. This result is an unhappy (but good) staff member.

• Another principle that we should heed is the Peter Principle that states, *"In a hierarchy, every employee tends to rise to his level of incompetence"* (Laurence J. Peter). In this sense, both the employer and employee should be aware that when an employee is being promoted or placed in a position of greater responsibility for which he is not equipped, he will eventually reach a level of incompetence, as he is unable to fulfill the demands or adjust to his new role and function. He becomes ineffective, not because he is a poor performer but because the shoes given to him are far too large for his feet. A significant gap exists between his current capability and the dimensions of his new position.

• Do not be afraid to hire someone who is better than you. When your people do well, you will do better; but when your people perform badly, you will become the biggest loser. Everyone has his or her own set of competencies and skills, and we are to leverage on each other's strength to grow and to achieve the organization's vision. Do not make the mistake of trying to wrestle with your innate inabilities, holding on to them for fear of letting others know or see them. Let go by getting others who are skillful to support you where you are weak. Your task is to nurture and strengthen whatever your skills and competencies.

> **As iron sharpens iron,**
> **So one man sharpens another.**
> **— Proverbs 27:17, NIV**

- Someone else's strength will offset your weakness and vice versa. Do not allow any inner sense of insecurity to lead you to feel threatened. Put on your PMA cap and channel the energy of your mind to gladly accept and learn from each other and to tap into each other's strength and abilities for mutual advancement and growth.

> **Some of my best thinking**
> **has been done by others!**
> **— John Maxwell**

- Getting the right person for the job will enhance your position and authority. The right person with the right character and competency will drive the business forward for you. You will then be able to focus your time, energy, and expertise to develop and pursue your other goals and plans.

- Focus on what you do best, and let others who are good in their areas of expertise do the rest. Remember, your objective is to achieve the desired results for which you have set your heart. Provide work plans with clear objectives, expectations, targets, and timing to ensure delivery of results. Review progress with the staff periodically.

> # Input influences outlook, outlook influences output, and output determines outcome.
> ## — Anonymous

 ## A Case Study on Character and Competency

This is a case of a staff member who displayed good values but had problems meeting one of his core responsibilities.

Thomas was a natural cheerleader. His bright and encouraging disposition would often spur his teammates to win. He had a good sense of humor and was able to garner support and commitment from his teammates. His teammates would usually nominate him to spearhead projects because they loved and enjoyed his style of leadership. He was full of energy and creativity and endeavored to make everyone happy in the workplace.

However, Thomas could not excel in his job. He was unable to produce the desired results set for him despite having been trained, coached, and equipped to handle the job. He could not fulfill his tasks efficiently. However, the position he held was the only job available to him in the organization.

Thomas was a classic case of not having the right competency for the job although he was a positive presence for his teammates. He could brighten up the workplace and get everyone moving. A decision had to be made by the management to retain Thomas or remove him.

What would you do if Thomas was your direct report?

During a half-yearly job appraisal and review of his progress, Thomas finally made the decision to leave the organization. The management accepted his decision.

As a result of his leaving the organization, team morale went down. Gone was the laughter and fun. There was no one as good as Thomas at cheering up the team when the going got tough. The organization's work climate had shifted in a significant way.

What would you have done?

Leaders must always take calculated risks, not only in terms of business decisions but also in people management. Leaders must look at the big picture and envisage the long-term effects and consequences of any decision they make, for today's decision will determine and affect tomorrow's results.

Often leaders have to make tough decisions, but it would help if they based their decisions on strategic pragmatism. Leaders must recognize different contributions made by their people. If a negative output has far-reaching effects and greater impact than a positive contribution, a decision has to be made to remove the negative output.

Let us take another example. James was a salesperson who often achieved his targets. He was considered a high performer who contributed to the overall organization's sales figures. However, he was not a team player; he caused strife among his colleagues.

In such a situation, would you retain a high performer and compromise on his negative character or remove a high performer because you value character above performance?

Remember, a drop of black ink will dispel the purity of clear crystal water in a jug. A little poison consumed over a long period of time will eventually damage the organs of a strong body.

To build an excellent team, every individual counts. Performance and character go hand-in-hand. They should come together as one package!

> **A sound body is a first-class thing;**
> **a sound mind is an even better thing;**
> **but the thing that counts for most**
> **in the individual**
> **as in the nation, is character,**
> **the sum of those qualities**
> **which make a man a good man and**
> **a woman a good woman.**
> **— Theodore Roosevelt**

LIVING THE CORE VALUES • CREATE FUN @ WORK

**Inspired
@
Workplace**

My MAD notes...

_____

_____

_____

_____

_____

_____

_____

_____

_____

_____

_____

_____

Key 1: I Am Important to the Company!
Key 2: Love Thy Neighbor
Key 3: Build Character & Competence, C & C

**INSPIRE POSITIVE CHANGE & GROWTH
CELEBRATE ACHIEVEMENTS**

How can I instill
Inspired @ Workplace?

_____

_____

_____

_____

_____

_____

_____

_____

_____

_____

TODAY'S LEADER IS HERE TO SERVE. THEN AND ONLY THEN WILL YOU BE SERVED.
ACCORDINGLY, BE THE FIRST TO HONOR, AND THEN YOU WILL ALSO BE HONORED.

If a man is called to be a street-sweeper,
he should sweep streets even as
Michelangelo painted, or
Beethoven composed music, or
Shakespeare wrote poetry.
He should sweep streets so well
that all the host of heaven and earth
will pause to say,
here lived a great street-sweeper
who did his job well.

— Martin Luther King Jr.

MAD

@

Workplace

"I was very passionate about being **MAD** in my work and with my customers. I breathed, slept, and ate **MAD**; thinking of ways to achieve that passionate desire **to make the difference**, and how willing I would be to make sacrifices for it.

— A **MAD** sales executive

1

Challenge the Status Quo!

Identify Challenges

Frame the challenges as opportunities for personal and organizational growth. Opportunities often come in the form of challenges. Also, when problems come your way, see opportunities in them and rather than seeing them as problems knocking on your door!

Each problem has hidden in it an opportunity so powerful that it literally dwarfs the problem. The greatest success stories were created by people who recognized a problem and turned it into an opportunity.
— Joseph Sugarman

Challenge the Status Quo

Get out of your comfort zone. Take on stretchable but attainable challenges. Stretchable challenges are in themselves an impetus to drive your inner strength and desire to rise above self to perform beyond the ordinary. Remember, it is always within your power to act for your long-term best interests.

When you want something you have never had,
you have got to do something you have never done.
— Mike Murdock

Be Courageous

Step out from your boundaries or pre-set limitations. Move faster, but sustain yourself at a comfortable pace. It takes more energy and time when you have to go backward and redo something you did not do well the first time because of hastiness and negligence.

Man cannot discover new oceans
until he has courage to lose sight of the shore.
— Thomas Edison

Set Priorities

Since the only thing that is constant is change, always consider present and immediate as well as future conditions and circumstances when setting priorities. Let those set priorities determine each step ahead.

Change is the law of life,
and those who look only to the past or the present
are certain to miss the future.
— John F. Kennedy

Be Prepared Mentally and Emotionally

Not everyone is tuned to changes and big dreams. Some may welcome changes, but many will resist them. You must strengthen yourself emotionally and mentally before you make hard decisions that may not necessarily be popular with everyone in your team.

> **It often requires more courage to dare**
> **to do right than to fear to do wrong.**
> **— Abraham Lincoln**

Be Enterprising

You have a stake in the company! If you are a staff member, think, talk, and act like the owner or the founder of the organization. Your workplace is the best available opportunity for you to utilize your talents, skills, and competencies to prepare and equip you for your future ventures. Do not engage in a narrow-thinking path that says, *"This is not my company. If I give all my best, the company benefits, but not me!"*

Remember, you receive wages to perform to the expectations of your organization. But you are paid to learn and contribute, not only toward the organization but also toward your future endeavors! Start putting on your entrepreneurial cap! This is your business.

How do you challenge your business to greater heights? You have a valuable stake in it, so be productive and bear good fruit for the sake of your own future!

> **Small opportunities are often**
> **the beginning of great enterprises.**
> **— Demosthenes**

Being passionate means possessing
an intense, burning affection that comes
with courage, perseverance, and endurance
to overcome all odds.
To be **MAD**, passion must be part
of our personae because passion
makes us love what we do
and when we do,
we do it differently.

Fire up Your Spirit and Imagination!

Be Passionate and Love What You Are Doing

Strong passion brews the most beautiful aroma of perfection. The intense desire to see a beautiful ending will point the way to produce good work.

Be Inspirational

Watch how the birds fly freely in the sky. Engage your heart, energize your mind, and challenge your creative spirit to the furthest shores of your imagination! Let your spirit flow. A free spirit generates a creative and innovative mind. Engage in techniques that can effectively unlock your creativity.

> **Creativity is the natural extension**
> **of our enthusiasm.**
> **— Earl Nightingale**

Build Your Ideas and Concepts around People's Desires

Know your customers' hearts' desires and what arouses those desires. Understand their inspirations and what stimulates their souls. Find out what drives them to act and what their aspirations and ambitions are. What are their unspoken wants?

Incorporate all these in your execution. This is the door to your customers' hearts!

Do Not Resist Bold Ideas

Often, extraordinary ideas require some changes in the way we conduct our normal business. Occasionally it demands a break of our workflow pattern. Though the idea can bring the improvement or result we desire, the change that comes with the idea is often resisted because of fear of the unknown. Have no fear of the unknown because it *is* unknown!

> **Many of our fears are tissue paper-thin,**
> **and a single courageous step**
> **would carry us clear through them.**
> **— Brendan Francis**

Be an Innovator

Set your mind free to generate fresh concepts. Create wants and needs in the hearts and minds of people. Inspire them with good reasons to believe that your innovations meet their needs and unspoken wants. Gather as many ideas and concepts as you can from everywhere and from people from all walks of life. Work with your customers, your advertising agency, your public relations firm, your brand consultants, your suppliers, and your colleagues.

The entrepreneur finds a need and fills it.
The innovator anticipates or
creates a need and fills it.
— Denis E. Waitley and Robert B. Tucker

Enlarge Your Imagination

Expand your paradigm. Remove all limits and doubts from your mind. View things differently, from different angles and perspectives. There are times when you have to see things through the eyes of an excited child. Perceive and survey the end result; see what you are capable of producing and multiplying. Look through a magnifying glass or a telescope to explore the unseen potential of an idea or prospect. Do not be short-sighted. Often you have to maneuver a raw idea before transforming it into bold actions. Strive for new, different, and better ways of doing things.

Never expect a 16" x 20" idea
to be celebrated by a 3" x 5" mind.
— Mike Murdock

I have learned that success
is to be measured not
so much by the position that
one has reached in life
as by the obstacles
which he has overcome
while trying to succeed.

— Booker T. Washington

3

Expect Outstanding Results!

Define What Constitutes an Outstanding Result and What It Means to You

Ask:

- *What do I need to do right now to achieve the maximum positive results?*
- *What is the gap between where I am now and where I want to be?*
- *How and what should I do now to erase this gap to reach the other end?*

Specify timeframes to accomplish your plans and to achieve the desired results in your work. Setting a deadline often unlocks the creativity and resourcefulness within you.

To achieve excellent results:

➤ Always position your thinking and emotions on the right platform, right channel, and right frequencies;

➤ Be discerning and disciplined with where you invest your energy and resources and in your choices or selections of ideas, plans, people, or resources with which to work;

➤ Engage everything with a resourceful mind; deploy your current best resources to meet your objectives;

➤ Release your thinking "antennae" to search for new concepts and solutions no matter what obstacles may come to confront you.

Pursue Excellence

In your pursuit of excellence, you will surely encounter difficulties. Grow wise from these difficulties! You become better and more equipped with each attempt, and you will learn from the error of your ways.

Divide the difficulties into smaller issues, or re-shape the difficulties into manageable issues. Keep sharpening your intelligence, skill, and competency, for until you have done something beyond what you have already mastered, you have not scaled greater heights or achieved higher platforms of success.

> **The quality of a person's life is in direct proportion to their commitment to excellence, regardless of their chosen field of endeavor.**
> **— Vince Lombardi**

Never Give In!

Be diligent and persevere. Do not be complacent and compromise with lower standards or settle for second-class honors. All excellent work comes with ease after we have learned to work harder and smarter each time.

The more you are willing to keep up your pursuit, the greater the force and strength to get what you want to get, the more triumphant will be your victory!

Outstanding results do not come overnight. They are not presented to you on a golden platter. Remember not to let short-term obstacles prevent you from pursuing and achieving your long-term goals. Nothing extraordinary comes easy, but it will surely come when you keep believing and pursuing it with great passion, focus, and faith.

> **Never give in, never give in,
> never, never, never, never—
> in nothing, great or small, large or petty—
> never give in except to
> convictions of honor
> and good sense.**
> — Sir Winston Churchill

BE INSPIRED • BE PASSIONATE • BE ENTERPRISING

MAD
@
Workplace

My MAD notes...

_____

_____

_____

_____

_____

_____

_____

_____

_____

_____

Key 1: Challenge the Status Quo!
Key 2: Fire up Your Spirit and Imagination!
Key 3: Expect Outstanding Results!

ENLARGE YOUR IMAGINATION • EXPAND YOUR PARADIGM

How can I be
MAD @ Workplace?

_____

_____

_____

_____

_____

_____

_____

_____

_____

_____

KEEP SHARPENING YOUR INTELLIGENCE, SKILL, AND COMPETENCY, FOR UNTIL AND UNLESS YOU HAVE DONE SOMETHING BEYOND WHAT YOU HAVE ALREADY MASTERED, YOU HAVE NOT SCALED GREATER HEIGHTS OR ACHIEVED HIGHER PLATFORMS OF SUCCESS.

When you're deeply into **MAD**,
your work will never be the same.
You will strive to **make a difference**
in everything you aim to do.
Nothing can really stop you!
By all means you will find ways
to get it or to get there.
My customers love me
because I am **MAD** in their business!

— A **MAD** salesperson

The Third Building Block ...

MAD

@

Marketplace

They are not "risk focused";
They are
"opportunity focused."
— Peter Drucker

Seize Opportunities.
Be Opportunity Focused.

Generate Insights from Outside, but Digest and Execute the Insights from the Inside Out

This is not just an intellectual process but comes from the depths of your emotional intelligence. Identify, perceive, and mull over the insights using both the right and left sides of your brain.

Ask Clever Questions that Draw Answers from the Heart and Mind

Seek valuable knowledge and understanding from multiple sources with the purpose of producing the desired fruits. Probe situations objectively without being prejudiced so you can identify and capture potential opportunities. Question uncertainties to affirm your thoughts and plans. Consider all possibilities, for everything is possible.

Be Opportunity Focused

Do not sit on good ideas or procrastinate over the next appropriate action to take when you know that an excellent idea is within your grasp. Do not forego opportunities at your doorstep. Often we are the ones that forfeit ourselves from receiving blessings.

Learn to Discern and Practice Self-Control and Discipline

Let go of what is not beneficial and that which does not serve your goals. Often we choose to hold on to what we have been (busily) doing, not because it brings more and higher value but because we fear embarking on a new idea would demand a change in the way we do business or that it takes away a certain sense of pride or detracts from a work culture. We are not willing to forego current business concepts, structures, experiences, comforts, or enjoyment for better things in the long run, sometimes even when an impasse is reached. We want to keep the status quo, and at the same time, we want extraordinary achievements. This formula does not work. Albert Einstein said:

> The significant problems we face
> cannot be solved at the same level
> of thinking we were at
> when we created them.

Similarly, we cannot attain extraordinary results if we remain at the same level of thinking and working as now. We must re-define what we are doing now and for the future if we want to create major growth opportunities.

See What (Opportunity) Is and Not What Seems to Be!

Know and be sure of what you are looking for so that when it comes, you are able to recognize it. Work on it immediately, and take advantage of the timing as well as the opportunity. Many good plans do not produce the right or desired results because of poor execution and/or timing. Do not launch a plan before or after its time. A fruit that is not ripe should not be eaten, for it will not be at its best. Similarly, an overripe fruit is unpleasant to taste. In the same vein, you must know the right or appropriate timing to launch your plans.

Raise questions on potential obstacles to the opportunities and frame or re-phrase them in such a way that they appear to be challenges that can be handled with ease and will produce the desired results.

> **Don't find fault.**
> **Find a remedy.**
> **— Henry Ford**

Be reminded that when facing critical issues or problems, it is wise to break them into smaller parts; work on each part by focusing on solutions and seeking potential opportunities; and then consolidate the solutions. You will find that issues or problems often lead you to a higher level of improvisation and excellence and provide you with more ground to reap opportunities.

> **Sometimes we stare so long at a door**
> **that is closing that we see too late**
> **the one that is open.**
> **— Alexander Graham Bell**

Be Watchful

Do not be led astray by competition or unforeseen changes in the market or unplanned situations. Attend to emergencies objectively and calmly, for they may lead you to big opportunities. You should always be watching from the top from where you will have a sharper, larger, and clearer view. While keeping your ears on the ground for accurate information, ensure that your thinking is pitched at the point of conclusion so you can envisage the results or outcome of each situation. This will enable you to capture potential opportunities and make brilliant decisions.

Plan and Prepare

Planning and preparation are critical and integral instruments for seizing opportunities. Without them, you are not ready to take on opportunities, even when they land on your lap. Remember the universal truth—as you sow, so will you reap. Therefore, if you do not give enough thought, care, and diligence to what you are doing now and for the future, you will reap fruit according to what you have planted.

Everything produces after its own kind. Much planning and preparation must be applied to the seeds and to the ground. The skill required to frequently plough the ground and the usage of the right tools are instrumental in cultivating the soil and ensuring that it is fertile before harvesting bountiful crops. Without proper groundwork, you will not be able to maximize or take full advantage of the benefits of your opportunities.

> Do not be deceived.
> A man reaps what he sows.
> Let us not become weary in doing good,
> for at the proper time
> we will reap a harvest if we do not give up.
> — Galatians 6:7, 9

Be Proactive and Not Reactive

Reacting to emergencies that have sprung from inefficiency, incompetence, or negligence drains your energy and enthusiasm. Look out, look forward, anticipate, and take action to realize and create growth opportunities.

> **Give me six hours to chop down a tree**
> **and I will spend the first four**
> **sharpening the axe.**
> **— Abraham Lincoln**

How you enter can decide how you exit.
Your exit will be remembered
longer than your entry.

— Mike Murdock

Reconnect with Your Customers

Study Your Customers

Do you know your customers' businesses intimately? What is the extent of your business relationship with your customers? Are you just another supplier to your customers, or are you your customers' preferred supplier and business partner?

Make every effort to know and understand the nature of your customers' businesses, especially their needs and wants. Listen to them. Hear them.

Know your customers' character and behavior—what they like and dislike.

Have reasonable knowledge about your customers' backgrounds—their families, education, hobbies, passions, and circle of friends.

Study your customers. Discern what they consider to be excellent customer service. Study their minds, and feel their heartbeat. Anticipate questions and objections. Understand your own sense of direction with each customer. What are the things that displease him? What reassures and pleases him when he is looking for a business partner?

Establish direct contact with your customers' team members and other personnel from within their organizations that influence the buying decisions. Do not neglect the storekeepers or warehouse (logistic) managers; they are often a valuable source of reliable information. You must establish touch points with every party or functional unit that has a say or a hand in your service or products.

Display Professionalism

When your customers speak, give them your total and absolute attention and focus. Lend an ear to what they have to say, discerning the spoken and unspoken.

Be tactful with your words and actions. Exclude negative or abrasive words and phrases from your vocabulary. Demonstrate respect to yourself and to your customers. Display professionalism and excellence in all things you undertake for them. Be consistent in your character and speech. Reflect your core values at all times.

It is imperative that you observe proper planning and preparation before meeting customers. To have no planning and preparation is to plan to fail. Great success is often the result of superior preparation but not excessive or hasty preparations.

Always keep yourself abreast of industry trends and developments. Ensure complete and accurate information. Be on ground to draw insights from customers and consumers, and put together plans for your customers in anticipation of changes in the market.

Know Your Competitors

Know the level of relationship your competitors have with your customers. Be friendly with your competitors. Do not condemn or criticize them in front of your customers. Remember, competition is good for every business. It challenges you to engage your creativity and intelligence in the search for ideas and solutions and enlarges your paradigm to consider other alternatives in delivering more excellence in your work. Your competitors are your benchmark for improvement and excellence. Understand their unspoken organizational limits. Anticipate their moves and their next course of action or plans with your customers. Then look for and preempt their moves.

> Whether it's Google or Apple or free software,
> we've got some fantastic competitors
> and it keeps us on our toes.
> — Bill Gates

Know Your Competitive Edge

What differentiates you from your competitors? How do your customers perceive you and your organization vis-à-vis your competitors? Emphasize your strengths and points of differentiation. Leverage them. Maximize them to reap maximum benefits, both for you and for your customers.

> It's through curiosity and looking
> at opportunities in new ways
> that we've always mapped our path at Dell.
> There's always an opportunity to
> make a difference.
> — Michael Dell

Loan your ears to your customers,
hear what is not spoken, and
acknowledge their hidden needs,
and you will immediately open
a pathway to their hearts.

3

Delight Your Customers!

Stop Selling!

Your task is to help your customers grow their businesses and profitability. You are a businessman, not a salesman. You are building a business, not a selling career. Your key task is to build and maintain sustainable customer relationships that bring mutual benefits for long-term growth.

Employ and maximize the benefits of your organization's points of differentiation that also form your cutting edge. Be consistently focused to deliver these points of differentiation to your customers. These points are your trademark! Your customers choose to buy from you because they believe and have confidence in the features and benefits of your trademark. They take delight in it. Only you and your organization can deliver your trademark benefits!

Never start anything with your customers if you have no commitment and intention to finish it well. Be disciplined, and do not to allow others or events to take you away from pursuing and achieving your goals. Remain focused on your objectives. Being disciplined is hard, but it is the bridge that links your objectives to your accomplishments.

Win Your Customers' Hearts and Minds

Work toward delivering a customer experience that wins hearts and minds. Intellectually connecting with your customers is not enough; you must engage them emotionally as well as connect with the thoughts within their hearts. Position yourself in the shoes of your customers; wear their thinking caps and put on their garments so you are able to comprehend and appreciate their demands, expectations, and desires. With these insights, you can then work toward plans and programs that meet and satisfy their intellectual and emotional needs.

> Mind to mind;
> heart to heart.

Do not compromise on anything that will discredit your integrity and reputation in favor of short-term needs or gains. It is said:

> The quality of your product will be remembered
> long after the price you charged for it is forgotten.
> But your integrity will always be remembered
> longer than your product.

Be Truthful

Always be truthful to your customers and deliver what you promise. In essence, what you say is what you deliver. Never misrepresent your organization or your products to your customers. Do not make excuses when you fail to deliver what you have promised, and never tell lies. When you lie, you often have to tell another lie to cover your tracks. In no time, you will be tangled in a web of lies, and you will likely be found out. On the other hand, when you tell the truth, you need not worry about remembering what you said because truth is constant and there is no effort needed in to remember truths. Hence, honesty is always the best policy. We acknowledge that sometimes it is difficult to be honest when circumstances are not favorable to you, but an honest relationship is worth more than the closure of a hundred deals. Ultimately, honesty always pays better.

> **Truthful lips endure forever,**
> **but a lying tongue lasts only a moment.**
> **— Proverbs 12:19**

When you make a mistake, be humble enough to admit it. Do not be defensive. Explain the situation politely and gently. When you try to defend your errors, it only suggests that your customer is wrong and you are right. Acting defensively will deter your customer from being receptive to you, and this will impact your ability to establish a fruitful relationship with your customer.

Anything that will bring about negative conclusions about you or your organization must be eliminated.

Have Integrity

Do not substitute integrity with persuasion or lies. To delight your customers is not to merely utter compliments or praise, especially where it is not due. Often, they want to be seen right even when they are wrong. However, that does not give you a reason to speak untruthful words to them. Customers are not foolish people. Your lack of integrity will ultimately destroy your credibility because customers judge your shallow words as empty verbiage whose sole intention is to manipulate or impress.

Remember, a man's word is his honor, for the words that flow out from the belly of his soul represent the character of the man.

> **As water reflects a face,**
> **so a man's heart reflects the man.**
> **— Proverbs 27:19**

Do not make any decisions or say things that are detrimental to your reputation and standing with your customers. Compromising your integrity is as good as losing your dignity. You will also lose everything you have worked for when you lose your credibility and reputation.

> **It takes twenty years to build a reputation**
> **And five minutes to ruin it.**
> **If you think about that,**
> **you'll do things differently.**
> **— Warren Buffett**

Remember, your customer chooses to buy what you are selling; therefore, your customer is incapable of being wrong. If he is wrong, then it is wrong that he bought from you!

Empathize with Your Customers

When your customers complain, always put yourself in their position and try to see their point of view so that you fully understand the nature of their complaints or problems. Acknowledge their feelings, but do not necessarily sanction their complaints. It is better that they complain to you about their dissatisfaction than to show indifference. This reveals that they do care about their business with you. Such a situation also gives you an opportunity to display your skill in problem-solving and relationship-building.

A customer who chooses to be apathetic to your products or level of service has decided that you and your organization are not worthy of his business and time. Once he secures another source of supply, he will drop you. It is always easier to maintain a customer's loyalty than to work to win back his or her confidence and goodwill.

Be Your Customer's Number-One Solution Provider

Bring to their table your creative ideas and concepts that will help to grow your customers' businesses. Be their business partner who provides them solutions to their needs.

Ask yourself this question: *"Am I my customers' number-one solution provider?"*

I firmly believe that any man's finest hour—
his greatest fulfillment to all he holds dear—
is that moment when he has worked
his heart out in a good cause
and lies exhausted on the
field of battle victorious.

— Vince Lombardi

Go Beyond Meeting the Customers' Requirements

Deliver Not Just What Is Required but What Is Desired

Don't just meet your quotas. Exceed your own expectations and your customers' expectations as well. Often customers will not tell you about specific problems or the solutions they are seeking. You have to listen with your heart and hear that which is unspoken. Anticipate what your customers want and hope to have. When you aim to exceed your set targets, it gives your creativity a chance to soar and to find extraordinary ways to delight your customers.

Go the extra mile for your customers, even if it requires you to do something that is beyond your job description—like buying a small gift for your customer's birthday. Be willing to do more than what is expected. It will surely help you reap better fruits from your labor. You will see that results are often commensurate with the extent of your efforts.

Let your customers be surprised when you deliver more and faster than you promised. However, do not over-commit yourself when you know you cannot deliver. When situations do not permit you to go beyond meeting your customers' needs, say no politely and in a pleasant way.

Create a Climate That Will Draw Your Customers to You

Be sensitive to your customers' needs. Have interpersonal sensitivity. Display a good sense of humor. Be enthusiastic and excited about being your customers' business partner. Bring fun and sunshine to your customers. Focus on delighting them every time you meet them. Think of how you can make a difference in their work and in their relationship with you. Aim to make their day!

Let your customers know that you appreciate their support. Reinforce that periodically. A simple handwritten card, a "get well" or a "thank you" note or some small tokens will make the difference!

Be Passionate about Your Customers!

Remember, in order to establish a solid business relationship with your customers that will survive through any tough times, you must look beyond the scope of their business or the conduct of normal business dealings. You must decide on the level or depth of the relationship you want to establish with your customers, and you must be prepared to deliver the required level of commitment.

> A lukewarm business relationship does not go far and will not produce or deliver the kind of growth for which you are aiming.

To be passionate about delighting your customers, you have to ask yourself these questions:

- *How else can I delight my customers?*

- *How can I be of greatest service to my customers?*

- *What do I need to do now to leave a distinctive mark of excellence on my customers?*

- *Am I MAD in my customers' lives?*

- *How can I make my customers love me?*

MIND TO MIND • HEART TO HEART

MAD
@
Marketplace

My MAD notes...

_____

_____

_____

_____

_____

_____

_____

_____

_____

_____

_____

Key 1: Seize Opportunities. Be Opportunity-Focused
Key 2: Reconnect with Your Customers
Key 3: Delight Your Customers!
Key 4: Go beyond Meeting Customers' Requirements

TOP-OF-THE- MIND * CORE-OF-THE-HEART

How can I be
MAD @ Marketplace?

_____

_____

_____

_____

_____

_____

_____

_____

_____

_____

_____

DELIVER NOT JUST WHAT IS REQUIRED BUT WHAT IS DESIRED.
WORK TOWARD DELIVERING A CUSTOMER EXPERIENCE THAT WINS HEARTS AND MINDS.
INTELLECTUALLY CONNECTING WITH YOUR CUSTOMERS IS NOT ENOUGH; YOU MUST ENGAGE THEM
EMOTIONALLY AS WELL AS CONNECT WITH THE THOUGHTS OF THEIR HEARTS.

are you mad?

The
MAD
Stories

Stories @ Workplace

Stories @ Marketplace

If history were taught in the form of stories,
it would never be forgotten.

— Rudyard Kipling, Nobel Prize 1907

Stories
@
Workplace

Sonya was a manager who joined the company several years before D. Lauren came on board. This is her story before the implementation of **MADBiz**.

I was one of the longest-serving staff members at the company. When I joined, the work culture was very different. Every department functioned as an individual unit. There was little interaction between departments or even among colleagues. Everyone practically worked in isolation. Often, the right hand had no inkling of what the left hand was doing and vice versa. Departments competed against each other instead of working toward common goals and objectives. Naturally, distrust and disagreement were commonplace. Often issues and problems were merely shoved aside, which led to a buildup of unresolved issues that eventually spilled over to affect our business. Customers grew increasingly dissatisfied, discontented, and disgruntled with our service. In turn, this deteriorating scenario disoriented and de-motivated our sales teams.

> **This 'out-of-sight; out-of-mind' approach led to a build-up of unresolved issues.**

During my early years, few of us had a true grasp of the company's goals and plans to realize these objectives. Information and communication from the leadership did not filter down effectively, so most of us did things our own way. In many instances, our attitude was "my way or the highway"! What made things worse was the environment in the office. There was an air of complacency and an attitude of indifference throughout the organization. There was very little warmth shown between coworkers. It was very much every man for himself and every woman for herself! It didn't take long for this atmosphere to poison our sense of purpose. We began to view our jobs merely as a means to earn a living as opposed to being an enriching and organic part of our lives. It was certainly no surprise that I found myself looking forward to going home as soon as I walked into the office! Very soon, we were like the black sheep of our huge conglomerate. This sense of low esteem made us feel alienated. Our desolation was obvious for all to see.

The sad fact was that we had lost passion for what we were doing, and the truth was that we did not love but needed our jobs!

> **The sad fact was that we had lost passion for what we were doing and the truth was that we did not love but needed our jobs!**

With the onset of SARS, things only became worse. The food and beverage industry, which we were in, was among the hardest hit by the impact of SARS. In the face of this, our flagging morale and brittle confidence simply went to pieces.

It was only when the new managing director came on board that the situation began to turn around. She brought with her a breath of fresh air and a whole new way of doing things. Imagine our shock when within a month after SARS, she announced three major exercises to rejuvenate the company. We almost fainted in disbelief! We could not believe she would be so bold as to institute a major restructuring exercise at such a critical period. There was a lot of skepticism, and people were saying that such actions were like digging our own graves! At that point, we could not see the light at the end of the tunnel.

After the implementation of **MADBiz** :

Far from the doom and gloom that we had predicted, the changes brought on by the managing director were indeed revolutionary. There was a dramatic change in every aspect of our work. The turnaround was remarkable. We saw and experienced firsthand the aggressive and bold changes taking place both in the workplace and in the marketplace. MADBiz *was hugely successful in turning around the company!* Everything changed, from our attitudes to our behavior! We became a cheerful, livelier, and more passionate lot. You could even say that we had been resurrected!

In the beginning, however, we had our doubts. We were still trapped by our old habits and a "cannot-do" attitude. Some salespeople could not accept the new vision and plans and resigned en bloc. We thought that was the end!

> We were still trapped by our old habits and a "cannot do" attitude.

But the managing director had a plan. She expected a measure of resistance to her style of business from both customers and the staff. But she had all the solutions in hand, and she was determined to push her agenda through.

She began by re-aligning our thoughts in line with the new vision. She constantly communicated with us. She kept us abreast of the latest developments and our progress. Throughout she kept reminding us that we were an important part of the business and that every staff member had an integral role in contributing to the realization of the company's goals. She made us feel involved in every aspect of the organization's growth. She encouraged our active participation in all company projects. She would walk around and talk to us instead of e-mailing or communicating over the telephone. She believed that face-to-face contact would lead to greater understanding for a better working relationship. She called it "walkabout, not armchair, management," and this was one of her favorite phrases!

I recall one instance when we came into the office to find that it was decorated with inspiring posters, and every table held a little flowerpot with personalized names and beautiful quotes. We had never experienced such an environment before! Across the wall, a big banner said, *"We are a winning team!"* Later, we found  out that our managing director had personally gone to the office over the weekend with her family members and friends to decorate the workplace for us. We were overwhelmed by her efforts to encourage us to move forward.

She called it "walk-about, not arm-chair, management".

D. Lauren told us in one of our meetings: "All of us here are standing on equal ground, and we will all start today and make a new ending, a triumphant ending! We will make a difference in the marketplace. But first, we have to make changes in our lives and in our workplace before we can make a difference in others' lives. And we will help each other to achieve this."

People remember us by what we do and not by what we say. What you say will be long forgotten but not what they see you do.

Time and again, D. Lauren would remind us, "Everyone must personify the core values because they are what we stand for and believe in as the winning team. There is no point saying that I care when I don't really care. Sooner or later, others will see through our hypocrisy. Always keep this in mind that people remember us by what we do and not by what we say. What you say will be long forgotten but not what others see you do."

And she practiced what she preached. She would greet us each day by saying, "Good morning, winning team!" She made a point that a winning team was not just about competence, but more importantly, it was about developing character! She introduced core values into our work culture, values like being passionate and loving what we do, being compassionate, sharing, and being courageous enough to make a difference.

> "... being good coaches and mentors to them so that they can succeed and win by themselves."

And D. Lauren told team leaders, "Leadership is not just about teaching or telling your team members what to do so they follow your instructions but being good coaches and mentors to them so that they can succeed and win by themselves."

D. Lauren strongly believed in learning from the lives and experiences of others whether they had failed or succeeded in their endeavors. She used to encourage us to read books to gain more understanding and wisdom about life. She would say, "What is $70 to pay for a book when you can learn and acquire wisdom and insights from the author, who went through perhaps a lifetime of experiences to learn and discover him or her? Seventy dollars is all you pay to help you avoid certain pitfalls or to remind yourself not to repeat the mistakes of those who tasted them. Seventy dollars is such a small investment to improve your life!"

On another occasion, she emphasized the importance of acquiring "emotional quotient." She said, "Yes, it is good to have high IQ, and you will be admired by many, but when you have high EQ, everyone is drawn to you! EQ attracts. It is like a magnetic force that draws additional, much-needed support and strength from people around you to keep you strong, confident, and going."

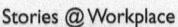

To encourage a culture of learning and development, she set up a mini-library for the staff! She would take time to scout around for the right books for all levels of staff, whether it was books pertaining to work function, careers, or personal development. There were even books on creative art and mind mapping, humor, and famous quotes as well as on relationships, such as *Men are from Mars and Women are from Venus* and *The 5 Languages of Love!*

It didn't take long for the marketplace to react to the three major exercises introduced by D. Lauren. It is a natural instinct to resist change. As expected, our customers were up in arms, with our sales team bearing the brunt of their displeasure and discomfort. Here, our managing director showed us what true leadership is all about. Instead of letting her subordinates take the heat, she put herself on the firing line. During these times, she often brought with her managers and executives from other organic departments that ordinarily don't deal directly with our customers. They included personnel from customer service, finance, and marketing. In this way, she ensured that

whenever there was an issue with, say, marketing, the marketing team would be there to work it out with the customer. If it was an accounting issue, the finance team would be there to deal with it immediately. Likewise, if there was a delivery problem, the customer service manager would be at the customer's doorstep. Everyone was involved!

I recall an incident when a highly unhappy wholesaler confronted D. Lauren during one of our market visits. It was clear that he intended to embarrass our managing director in front of her team. He called her a potato, which in the local dialect refers to a fool. The wholesaler raised his voice, shouting, "I guarantee that in no time, you will pack your bags and go home! You think your plans will work here in this country! I'm telling you now if you don't know! You will fail … you hear me? Fail!"

"I'm telling you now if you don't know! You will fail... you hear me? Fail!!!"

All of us were taken aback, and there were a few who took a step backward in the face of this onslaught. What came after was a surprise. D Lauren turned to us and said, "It's okay. I understand his frustration. It is good that he is being open to me. I welcome every gesture that has good intentions. Let him pour out his frustrations. He has taken the time to speak to me, and I will listen to him. By the way, I love eating potatoes."

Turning to the wholesaler, she then addressed him, saying: "I'm very happy to meet you. Thank you for taking the time to speak to me. I'm really sorry for making you so angry. I really would like to listen to you more. When I understand your problems, then I can help you. I sincerely want to support you. That's why I am here to see you personally. We both want to grow our businesses. You are very experienced in this field. I would like to hear you out. However, if you are not ready now … it's okay. I will come again next time. Thank you so much."

We succeeded in capturing the hearts and minds of our customers with our passion, perseverance, integrity and courage.

Her consolatory words had an immediate calming effect. His face relaxed noticeably, and he then invited us to sit down and discuss his issues. Ironically, this disgruntled wholesaler eventually became one of our biggest customers!

Within five months, events had taken a dramatic turn. We succeeded in capturing the hearts and minds of our customers with our passion, perseverance, integrity, and courage. The customers saw that we were genuinely interested in helping their businesses grow, and they were delighted.

Sometime later, creative posters began appearing in our office. They were everywhere—in the pantry and even in the washrooms! The posters carried slogans like:

WE ARE MAD!
WATCH OUT! MAD PEOPLE ARE HERE!
WE LOVE TO BE MAD!
WE ARE MAD EVERYWHERE!
THE MAD PEOPLE, THE WINNING TEAM!

What was going on? Had our managing director gone MAD??

Our staircase was painted with bold colors with the words, *"Making a difference in the workplace and in the marketplace"* painted on the steps!

MAD was no longer just a word to us; it was our culture. It was part of us, and it defined our lives!

We eventually realized that MAD is making a difference! Since our embrace of the MAD culture, we have grown stronger and created many MAD concepts and business programs for our customers. Twice a year, the whole team makes a visit to our customers and surprises them with games and presentations. Our customers have grown to look forward to our visits. We were definitely making a big difference in the marketplace!

Coming to work also became a much-anticipated daily event. We felt empowered. It was not just a job anymore. This was now a fun place to be, an environment that inspired us to live our lives differently. MAD was no longer just a word to us; it was our culture. It was part of us, and it defined our lives!

The core values were a big part of our MAD culture. D. Lauren made it a point to remind us to put it into practice. Eventually, she said, they would evolve into a habit.

Sure enough, the impact of living our core values within the workplace soon spilled over to the marketplace. Our customers, naturally, were pleasantly surprised. At times it amazed me to see how customer service could attend to angry customers with sugary sweet tones in their voices!

Customer service could attend to angry customers with sugary sweet tones in their voices!

Like all workplaces, petty arguments arising from misunderstandings or miscommunications are commonplace. How we choose to resolve them is a mark of leadership.

We had a case where two managers were engaged in a cold war. D. Lauren stepped in and told them both, "Let me share a true story. My parents had five children, all daughters. When I was very young, my mom called all the five daughters together and asked each of us to look at our right palm with our five fingers pointing out. She said her five daughters were like the five fingers; each finger has its own unique character and function. When the individual fingers work together in harmony, they do great stuff. Then she would ask us to bite every finger! Then, she explained that every bite caused the same amount of pain. That's because no one finger is less important than another."

"Similarly, as team leaders, whatever we do affects the whole team and the organization. I've heard both sides of your stories. I don't want to judge who is right and who is wrong. As far as I am concerned, both of you are in the wrong because both had failed to live out your core values! You are good leaders, but you have allowed your pride to stand in your way."

You are good leaders but you have allowed your pride to stand in your way.

Chastened, the two managers realized that her words rang true. It didn't take long for them to reconcile their differences!

Before she left the organization, D. Lauren shared a story with us that I can still remember till this day: "My ex-boss once told me, 'You see the chair I'm sitting on? Today, everyone says yes to me because I'm sitting on this chair. But if tomorrow I'm gone from this chair, will they still greet me warmly and say yes to me? Will they still support me as they used to when I sat on this chair? Will the suppliers continue to knock on my door? Life is such that when you have the power, position, and authority to lead and to command, people will submit to you, but the question is, are they submitting to you willingly from their heart because of your good leadership or because you can offer them what they want?'"

Are they submitting to you willingly from their heart because of your good leadership or because you can offer them what they want?"

Referring to this story, she then told us: "Regardless of whether you're holding a high position of authority or a lower position, what type of leader are you? When you leave your position, don't you want people to remain there for you simply because they have been inspired by you and your leadership?"

> **Never try to cover up your mistake when it is your mistake!**

Accountability was another value held in high regard by D. Lauren. There was a case where a senior staff member had mistakenly given an incorrect brief to a supplier. When the mistake was discovered by our managing director, the manager in question suggested that he would inform the supplier that the order had to be changed due to a shift in business strategy. He was reluctant to own up to his gaffe. D. Lauren would have none of it! She said: "Never try to cover up your mistake when it is your mistake! There's nothing wrong with owning up to your mistake. You can find solutions to rectify the mistake. But if you deny or do not want to face up to the truth of the matter or lie about your mistake, you will surely be hit with more mistakes and problems. It doesn't mean that if it is a supplier, it's okay not to admit your mistake since they need your business. You must not manipulate your supplier to get your wrong job done free. Why should they bear the cost of your mistake? Likewise, don't think we can lie to our customers too! Do you know the meaning of credibility and integrity? And do you know why I am telling you all this? I want you to be respected by your suppliers! So go tell the supplier the truth, and pay him

for the job he has done."

Being MAD was also about having fun at work. Fun at work is much more than just the physical appearance of the office environment. It is about enjoying your work and loving what you are doing. It is about building a workplace with a strong spirit of unity and harmony.

> **Being MAD was also about having fun@work.**

As a result of our MAD business approach and winning attitude, we won several regional and global awards. We also received public praise from our key customers. Our sales team was acknowledged as the best in town!

We felt important at our workplace. We knew we had contributed to the success. Our esteem was renewed. Our confidence was at an all-time high. We began to feel a deep sense of pride in being a part of the organization. We were no longer losers. We were now the winning team!

THIS MAD CULTURE REALLY
CHANGED MY LIFE.
THE GREAT PASSION MOVES
EVERYONE TO MAKE A DIFFERENCE
IN THEIR OWN LIVES AND
TO THE LIVES OF THEIR COLLEAGUES.
THE COMPANY REALLY
SPURRED ME TO LEAP FORWARD
AND BE EQUALLY MAD.
I FEEL GREAT BEING MAD!
IN THE END, OUR PASSION FOR
MAKING A DIFFERENCE
BECOMES AN INSPIRATION
TO OTHERS.

Another Story

By Mark, a new sales staff member who joined the organization after the implementation of **MADBiz:**

Most people only experience a culture shock when they travel abroad. In my case, joining the company was like going to another planet, as the people and work environment were unlike anything I had ever come across. Simply put, they were MAD! The mood was infectious, and before I knew it, I was just like them and loving it!

One of my first experiences at the company involved a workshop on how to create different but delightful experiences for our customers. I fully expected to sit behind a table and spend hours listening to presentation after presentation before the inevitable discussions and brainstorming sessions. What I found instead was the exact opposite. Instead of chairs and tables, the room was filled with toys, and we were asked to sit on the floor. Imagine that! A bunch of middle-aged executives sitting cross-legged like young children at preschool! And instead of formal discussions, our managing director opened with, "Let's have a fun time! You are free to choose whichever toy you want. Now go and choose your toys!"

That was effectively my introduction to how D. Lauren conducted fun @ work and gave me an insight into how totally MAD she was! Far from being a waste of time, the workshop set the stage for bringing passion and excitement into the workplace. And this in turn, spurred a free flow of ideas when it came to creating radically different experiences for our customers.

A few days later, I shared a conversation with a few colleagues about the toys. It was here that I learned more about D. Lauren, her outlook in life, and of course, her connection with toys!

Growing up in an impoverished family, she missed out on the normal pleasures of childhood. Unlike many of her schoolmates—who were relatively well to do—she didn't have the means to attend parties because her family could not afford presents. Her only toys were the ones she made, like dolls from scraps of paper. When she saw her friends or neighbors playing with toys, she would leave immediately to avoid the empty feeling of not being able to play with one once she got home. When D. Lauren became a mother, she resisted buying toys for her daughter because she assumed her daughter would be as immune to toys as she had become. But when she eventually brought one home, D. Lauren saw an outpouring of pure joy from her daughter, who was by then already ten years old!

One even spat at me! Another would turn his back to talk to me rather than do it face-to-face!

D. Lauren's "toy story" is perhaps the reason why she has such inner strength and the sheer willpower to rise above all challenges and obstacles in her life!

She brought this desire to excel into the workplace, and it certainly rubbed off on those around her. Like D. Lauren, my colleagues seemed similarly driven. Even for such events as our annual dinner attended by other subsidiaries of our conglomerate, we worked hard to produce the best and most creative presentation! Needless to say, we would always steal the limelight! We were truly a MAD team!

It was this attitude and passion that helped me to ride out the first difficult months at the company. As a salesperson, I noticed at the outset that many of our customers were openly hostile toward us.

 One even spat at me! Another would turn his back to talk to me rather than do it face-to-face! Yet I persevered in the face of such adversity, heartened and encouraged by the support shown by D. Lauren and the rest of the management team.

Our new sales team took on the moniker of "The Commandos." And they were true soldiers to the cause! We had two female members who didn't drive (they didn't have drivers' licenses!) but gamely walked from customer to customer in high heels carrying an assortment of promotional and other relevant materials. And they didn't even break a sweat! It was simply amazing! I wasn't surprised when they would consistently top the sales figures. These two were inspirational, and I told myself, *If they can do it, why can't I? If they can be MAD with their customers, so can I!*

 We were guided and inspired by an excellent mentoring and coaching system within the company.

We were guided and inspired by an excellent mentoring and coaching system within the company. We had leaders we could approach anytime. They led the teams by demonstrating the right leadership values and taught us the importance of leading by example.

D. Lauren joined me on one of my earliest sales calls. I was then struggling to connect with some of our wholesalers. On this occasion, one wholesaler decided to vent his frustration on us. With his son in attendance, he ranted and raved for a good fifteen minutes in his local dialect, never allowing us to get in even a single word! I suspect he only stopped because he was thirsty! It was at this point that D. Lauren—who doesn't speak the dialect—turned to me and said, "Please tell him I am sorry I cannot communicate in his dialect. But I can see he is excited to share with us about growing his business and the ways we can support him. Please tell him that we sincerely want to support his business. We are here to rectify whatever past issues we had. But I really would like the opportunity to explore these issues. Will he allow me to speak to him in English and you translate for me, or maybe I will try to speak in simple Mandarin if he doesn't mind?"

The angry wholesaler had become a happy wholesaler!

The wholesaler's son addressed his father, saying in their dialect, "You spoke so angrily for so long, but she did not understand you at all. You know what she said, right! She sounds sincere and wants to sort out your complaints. She's the boss, but she's here to talk to you! And she wants to see how to support our business. I will talk, and you can talk in Mandarin." The wholesaler reluctantly nodded his head and said: "Okay! See what she has to say. Anyway, she still smiled at me even after I told her off!"

It turned out to be a fruitful discussion, and at the end of it, there were smiles all round. The angry wholesaler had become a happy wholesaler!

After we left, I asked D. Lauren, "Do you want me to tell you what the wholesaler said in his dialect?" She laughed and said, "Mark, I understood what he said! I can understand his dialect, though I cannot speak it. The important thing is to turn the situation around and show them that we are different, that we are sincere, passionate, and serious about supporting them and growing our businesses with them. There is always a door of opportunity to be opened, but we are not aware of it  because at most times, our eyes are fixed on other doors that are shut to us. If the door is not there, then create that door! Always focus on the purpose and objectives of being there. Don't be distracted or derailed by peripheral issues."

During my time there, we had what D. Lauren called inspirational days, which were a platform to share and learn from each other. All of us were given the opportunity to present our own learning experiences.

> **There is always a door of opportunity to be opened but we are not aware of it because at most times, our eyes are fixed on other doors that are shut to us. If the door is not there, then create that door!**

D. Lauren placed a great emphasis on cultivating a learning culture within the organization. She ensured that those who went for training would share the knowledge and experience with the entire team.

I also recall another occasion when I learned about inspiring leadership from D. Lauren. We were waiting for her to announce which three members would be selected to attend Anthony Robbins's three-day seminar "Unleash Your Potential Within." We all expected the three to come from the sales or marketing teams. Instead, we were shocked when she picked them from our backend support operations! Two were from customer service and the other from finance! She then explained that battles are not won solely by those on the front lines but also by the support services. After all, they have to handle and process orders, deal with inquiries, and address problems to facilitate the work of the sales and marketing teams. The message was clear: It did not matter whether you were on the front lines or in the back rooms. She would recognize your efforts so long as you performed to the best of your abilities and had good character. All levels of staff are important stakeholders regardless of whether you are a senior manager or a junior staff member. Without every single staff member, the organizational structure would not be complete.

> **All level of staff are important stakeholders**

D. Lauren also made it a point to ensure that everyone lived the core values. On one occasion, she reminded her managers to include serving the cleaners or tea ladies food from the gatherings we had in the office. She once told a manager, "How would you like to work in an environment that is untidy and not clean or not have your rubbish bin cleared every day? Or how would you like it if the washroom was not cleaned every time? This is thanks to these cleaners who did their job well."

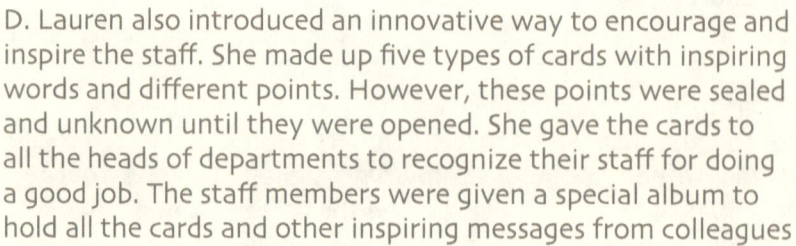

D. Lauren also introduced an innovative way to encourage and inspire the staff. She made up five types of cards with inspiring words and different points. However, these points were sealed and unknown until they were opened. She gave the cards to all the heads of departments to recognize their staff for doing a good job. The staff members were given a special album to hold all the cards and other inspiring messages from colleagues and management. At year's end, they would total the number of points received and be rewarded in kind according to the quantum. This initiative inspired every staff member to turn out his or her best performance. It was a creative and effective way to contribute toward the growth of the organization.

During my time in the company, my colleagues became my extended family. We turned to each other for support and inspiration. The leaders set the perfect example. We were truly a MAD family!

> **MAD gives me tremendous pleasure because I see my way of life change for the better. It gives me a great sense of fulfillment. I never imagined I would be able to touch many lives. MAD makes me feel I am created for a purpose.**

Stories

@

Marketplace

The Story

By Elis, a sales executive.

D. Lauren was instrumental to the change in my career path, a switch that I eventually embraced like a duck to water! By nature I was very much an introvert who preferred to sit behind a desk and carry out my work anonymously rather than going out in the field. My managing director, however, had a different idea. She saw potential in me that others, and myself included, never even knew existed! She talked me into joining the sales team, a move that I was initially tentative to make but grew comfortable with over time.

It helped that the MAD culture had transformed the workplace into a family-like environment. I was working with a group of friends rather than colleagues. The core values became our way of life, and I could see it was having a chain effect. People were friendlier and more approachable. As a result, I began to enjoy my work.

After all, we were meant to be our customers' No. 1 Solution Provider!

As a sales executive, my responsibilities were to service existing customers, start new accounts, introduce new products, and provide solutions for customers. After all, we were meant to be our customers' number-one solution provider!

One of my first assignments was to manage the account of a five-star international hotel. The hotelier I had to deal with was an influential figure in the industry, but he had a fearsome reputation of being stern. He had already shut the door on us due to past experiences with our sales team. He refused any and all overtures from us to meet and repair our relationship.

After countless attempts, he eventually agreed to see me. But he was only willing to give me a ten-minute window! Naturally, I was excited, but this was tinged with a fair amount of anxiety. We would probably get only one shot at this! Of course, my superiors and colleagues spent considerable time prepping me for this appointment.

> **I want to have nothing to do with your organization!**

When the day arrived, my sales manager came with me to the meeting. The moment we stepped in to his office, it felt like we were in a concentration camp! From the get go, the hotelier didn't hold back, expressing his disappointment, anger, and frustration at our level of service. At the end of his fiery monologue, he told us sharply, "I want to have nothing to do with your organization!" And that was it. The meeting was over before I could even utter a single word! No words could accurately describe how I felt there and then!

Our managing director, however, didn't seem crestfallen over the inability to make headway with this hotelier. She simply would not give up. Under her direction, we made a huge thank you card to thank him for the opportunity and "words of advice"! D. Lauren also coached me on how to turn a negative situation into a positive one, saying: "What is his underlying message? Can you hear what he did not say? Look into his mind and listen to his heart, and you will be able to see the problem as an opportunity and a challenge. Become his number-one solution provider!"

From then on, I would visit his office quite frequently. I say office because I never got to meet with him. But what I did was leave with his secretary countless ideas, concepts, and proposals on how we could help him grow his business, as well as snippets of the latest industry news. Periodically I would also send him congratulatory messages on his and his hotel's many achievements. When a leading local newspaper wrote a story about the hotel, we cut it out and framed it for him.

> "What is his underlying message? Can you hear what he did not say?"

A few months passed. Then one day, he met D. Lauren at an industry event. He told her that he appreciated our efforts and admired our perseverance. He even mentioned the thank-you card in response to his tirade. But more importantly, he agreed to give our company a second chance! That was the turning point!

> It is not for the customers to create opportunities for us – we have to create them ourselves!

It was my first big score! I began to understand the real meaning of delighting my customers by creating experiences for them. To become a preferred solutions provider, I had to break away from traditional practices and conventional expectations. I had to shift my mindset from meeting customers' requirements to exceeding their expectations. It is not for the customers to create opportunities for us—we have to create them ourselves! As D. Lauren said, "Don't wait for good luck to come your way. Good luck is for you to create. Good luck is when you are ready and prepared for the opportunity when it strikes! Often we miss out on opportunities because we were not equipped or ready to receive it."

On another occasion, we launched a thematic campaign to promote a new premium tea product. This was a project that showcased the brilliance and effectiveness of MAD! This was the plan.

The campaign knocked their socks off!

During the launch event, the customers were spread out at tables while professional models paraded down the aisle dressed according to the attributes, color, and character of each tea variant. Meanwhile, team members at each table highlighted the features and benefits of the product to our customers. Other team members then presented a variety of recipes made from the tea at every table.

Following the launch, our campaign shifted to our customers' doorstep. On three consecutive mornings, the sales team paid a visit to their offices. On the first day, the customer was served an elegantly presented breakfast featuring one tea variant. He or she was presented with a specially designed newspaper carrying stories on the rich heritage of the brand and product. This was repeated on the succeeding two days with another variant and "newspaper."

Our approach was a personal but creative one.

The campaign knocked their socks off! Our customers were amazed at the lengths we would go to delight them. Our approach was a personal but creative one. It was an experience that they remember till this day!

Being passionate about MAD
has taught me
life's most important lesson,
that nothing is impossible
if you put your heart and mind into it.

Another Story ...

By Keith, a sales executive.

MAD was entirely new to me. The culture permeated through every nook and cranny at our office and was eventually ingrained in our DNA. By living our personal and professional lives according to MAD and its values, concepts, and way of thinking, we achieved results far beyond what we could have imagined. I was particularly bowled over by the strong learning culture and the "never give up" attitude.

It is not the size that counts. It is the People. It is YOU!

D. Lauren was inspirational. To this day, I can still recall her advice. On one occasion, she told us, "People say we can do all these great things because we are a smaller organization. But let us be truthful. It is not the size that counts. It is the people. It is you! It has to do with our efforts to practice the core values daily, our beliefs, and our commitment to live up to the values."

We must always be active participants, and not mere spectators.

"We must always be active participants and not mere spectators. All of us want to live in a better world. All of us desire to be better people. That's the world we aim for in this organization. But we must work at it. Don't be afraid to be agents of change! Change empowers you to be different. Lead the change if you want to see it happen!"

Spurred on by her words, I was determined to make a difference, to be my customers' preferred supplier.

I found myself with a daunting challenge to win over a customer who had already forged a close working relationship with another supplier. The only thing I could get from him was a polite, "Thank you but no thanks!" response to my attempts to make inroads into his heart and mind. It would have been easy to let my head drop and admit defeat. But that wasn't the MAD way of doing business, so I soldiered on! I continued to pay him visits and give him samples of our products, complete with menu presentations. Though we were not chefs by profession, we were given kitchen and product applications training in order to present prepared recipes to customers for their tasting. Most times the customers were surprised to witness our passion and diligence to go the extra mile to impress them. Occasionally I would also slip in articles on his favorite sports. When he was under the weather, I sent him "get well soon" cards, along with natural remedies.

> No other supplier had ever been so attentive to his needs throughout his 30-year career.

This caught his attention because apparently, no other supplier had ever been so attentive to his needs throughout his thirty-year career.

My perseverance paid off. At first, his orders trickled in—a sample product here, another there. This soon turned into bulk orders, and he became one of my largest customers! And it didn't stop there, because he even introduced me to his business contacts!

Another of my customer was a five-star hotel with a rich heritage whose purchasing manager seemed to take pleasure in berating and belittling me. She would often hurl names at me like stupid and dumb. But what made it worse was that she refused to look at me in the eye! It was disconcerting to talk to someone who made it a point to stare at her computer screen without even so much as a glance at me.

> Now that you have my number right in front of you, you can call me any time when you need to complain or shout at somebody!

On one occasion, I gave her a clip-on stand to hold business cards. As expected, she launched into a sarcastic tirade about my company wasting money on "useless" gifts. As her voice grew louder, I clipped my business card on the stand and placed it next to her computer. For perhaps the first time ever, she turned her head toward me and seemed about to let loose another caustic string of insults. But before she could even start, I smiled at her and said, *"Now that you have my number right in front of you, you can call me any time when you need to complain or shout at somebody!"*

It worked! The beginnings of a smile appeared on her lips. Perhaps, I thought, it was merely a reflex action, but soon after that incident, she called and asked to see me. When I arrived, I was pleasantly surprised to see my clip-on stand still next to her computer with my business card prominently displayed! She asked me to submit a tender for a range of products her hotel needed, but added, "I don't

> I did not hire salesmen or saleswomen! I brought in businessmen and businesswomen to grow the business!

think your company will get the order. Your products are not suitable for our prestigious hotel!"

That was all the opening I needed! Back at my office, the entire sales team put our heads together to find the best and most effective way to present our products and their benefits. We didn't hold back and thought of a whole gamut of creative ideas to position our offering. The managing director chipped in with her thoughts: "Remember, I did not hire salesmen or saleswomen! I brought in businessmen and businesswomen to grow the business! This is your business! Now, ask yourself, how do I want to grow my business by leaps and bounds?"

We put emphasis on research and gathering "ground truth." We spent days at the hotel—dining in, observing their service, looking into the requirements in their kitchen and housekeeping, and understanding their specific needs and particular constraints. We then came up with several concepts and solutions, such as alternative packaging or supporting tools to facilitate housekeeping and kitchen chores, tailor-made attractive carriers to hold our products when serving guests, and also tying in theme promotions to some products that were supported by below-the-line advertising.

For us, it was always a "WIN-WIN-WIN situation". When our customer wins, the organization wins and I will also win!

Our efforts paid off, and we were awarded the order! We succeeded in selling not just products but also innovative ideas, concepts, and benefits and customized solutions. Over time, the purchasing manager in question became one of my most loyal customers!

It wasn't just the sales team who were coached on how to reconnect with customers. The coaching encompassed the entire organization. For us, it was always a "*win-win-win situation.*" When our customer wins, the organization wins, and I will also win.

> **We made it a point to impress on them that we were more than just a supplier. We were their long-term business partner!**

During my time in the company, we consistently worked toward differentiating ourselves from our competitors. We benchmarked against other FMCGs (fast-moving consumer goods) and not just our own industry. All our initiatives were designed to delight our customers and give them a superior experience. We made it a point to impress on them that we were more than just a supplier. We were their long-term business partner!

I was involved in another campaign to launch a new product. Here, we wanted to go the distance and make it an event that would live in our customers' memories forever. We wanted to communicate the features and benefits of the product creatively and persuasively instead of going the normal route with a product catalogue.

We produced a sixty-second TV commercial almost entirely through the efforts of the team. We were the cast, the crew, the scriptwriter, the director, and the producer. Everyone turned out to be intensely professional and responsible in their respective roles and functions. The production of the commercial was a great success.

We then set out to present the commercial at our customers' premises. Each of us carried a portable video player, which we would pull out from our bags and play for our customers and their staff members! It was a rare experience to see them light up on recognizing that the stars of the commercial were none other than the people who were holding the video players!

This is how we became their 'top-of the-mind' and core-of-the-heart'!

They were simply blown away by our passion to make a difference. The homemade commercial was a great starting point to make a pitch! It made everything else easy to do. We had won our customers' hearts by our MAD action. This is how we became their top-of the-mind and core-of-the-heart!

If I were not passionate and
serious about
making a difference in my job,
my customers would never
have trusted me with theirs!

The Closing Story ...

By Dean, a brand management executive.

As a member of the brand management team, I executed many marketing programs for the distribution channel with the goal of expanding product accessibility and visibility. Before MAD, I had never imagined that we would create such different and fun experiences for our customers. MAD @ marketplace took us into a whole new realm in brand building.

> **MAD@marketplace took us into a whole new realm in brand building.**

On one occasion, we decided to surprise our distributors, who were only looking to secure trade deals or bundle promotions from us. We came up with a brilliant but crazy idea! We made appointments with the distributors, informing them that we would drop by their offices to discuss business issues. They had no idea what was in store for them. Every one of us—from the managing director to the logistics staff—turned up at their doorsteps dressed as pop stars! We began playing music accompanied by different types of instruments. There was no doubt we caught our customers' attention! Their eyes and mouths opened and closed in disbelief! The team danced their way into their offices, and we performed songs and dances! Then one of our team members gave a speech on behalf of the organization, thanking them for their support and business partnership.

Our intention was to forge close ties with them. We wanted them to know they had a place in our family. From then on, our relationship with them was rock solid. This was an excellent brand-building exercise. It not only captured their attention, but it also heightened their awareness and affiliation for our brands. It was indeed an eye opener for me.

We applied the same principles at a product launch to our wholesalers. Our MAD plan took place right at their doorsteps. We turned up with our chefs and their equipment. The chefs cooked up a storm, and we served our customers with a magnificent presentation that included custom-made boxes, personalized names, and miniature samples of our new products, along with an attractive recipe booklet.

Everyone from our company was involved! It was a very personal launch done on a one-on-one basis. Needless to say, everyone immediately and happily signed up and placed orders! The wholesalers were so delighted with our creative yet very practical launch. Since then, they have always looked forward to further launches from us. And on our end, we continued to surprise them each time!

At another event for our commercial customers, we launched a product by inserting a miniature bottle of the item to fit into a mini-chef uniform measuring six inches tall and four inches wide, complete with their names embossed on the uniforms. It even came with a mini-hanger and a stopper to hang on a glass screen.

> We wanted them to know they had a place in our family.

We were driven by the MAD culture to deliver the difference to our customers. We believed not just in delighting our customers but also in going beyond to deliver not just what is required but what is desired.

MAD is not just about being different in our business offerings; it is also about creating and bringing fun to the customer's workplace. We wanted to share our values with our customers. We wanted them to remember us as a passionate team who believed in making the difference in and to their business.

> **We believed not just in delighting our customers, but also in going beyond to deliver not just what is required but what is desired.**

I remember this advice given by D. Lauren. She said, "We inspire each other to be MAD, and we are greatly inspired when we witness the fruits of our labor. We must recognize our role and contribution to the community. We must play our MAD part to remain relevant to our customers and to the industry as a whole. We give, and we receive. We receive, and we give. We sow, and we reap. We know when we inspire the industry, we are inspired to achieve greater heights and greater growth for the company. When the company performs well, we will also do very well. And so will our customers!"

During the International Chefs Day Celebration 2006, the team scripted a song and sung it in dedication to all chefs in Singapore. This was the song:

You Are a Star

A fire burning deep within your soul
You bring the world magnificence to behold
Your food creations never cease to inspire
The young
The would-be heroes who share your goal.

You give your heart, your spirit, yourself
You hold back nothing, a willingness to share
With rising stars, who'll carry on your glory
You are a star who all would like to be

CHORUS:

You are a star, a shining star so vibrant.
You are a star, a maestro of your domain.
Shining forth with vision and with passion,
You are a star,
With you there are no boundaries ...

Shining forth to conquer and inspire
You are a star, your passion never ends

END (VOICEOVER):

To the culinary stars,
chefs extraordinaire,
taking Singapore to international culinary glory,
we salute you!

For three consecutive years, we paid tribute to the food and beverage industry by celebrating their achievements in bringing home prestigious awards at international culinary competitions. Two years after SARS, we held a culinary extravaganza to pay tribute to Singapore's culinary masters.

The guests had a chance to taste the award-winning culinary masterpieces created and presented during the Igeho Salon Culinaire Mondial Switzerland 2005. For the first time, customers from all segments of the market and key personnel of the food and beverage industry came together to recognize and be recognized for their achievements and contributions. It was a night in which the who's who of Singapore's celebrated kitchens and famed F&B establishments exchanged their aprons for black ties alongside the economic captains of the industry. It was the biggest and most grand gala dinner a corporate organization had ever held for the food and beverage industry.

> This team is world class in terms of the service level they provide their customers. We are constantly delighted at what they do make us feel appreciated and important.

The dinner also saw the launch of Singapore's first-ever coffee table book profiling the movers and shakers and the venerable institutions of the local F&B industry. Entitled *Salut: A Taste for Excellence*, the coffee table book featured stories of more than thirty leading F&B personalities from hotels, restaurants, fast food chains, culinary institutions, master chefs, F&B

professionals, hospitality, housekeeping, and bartenders' associations. The book provided insights into their life stories, the practices of the industry, issues and challenges, and key developments.

Here are some of the comments for our efforts in this respect. The president of Singapore Chefs' Association (2005) said: "This team is world class in terms of the service level they provide their customers. We are constantly delighted at what they do make us feel appreciated and important. Each time I meet the team, it's amazing to see each and every one of them always smiling, and it makes customers feel good. They are very professional in the way they do business and when working with customers" (excerpt from *Hospitality Asia* magazine, Nov./Jan. 2006 issue).

> They also know how to mix fun with business which is important in today's hectic life.

We have achieved not only being our customers' preferred supplier but also an icon in the service industry, as stated by the president mentor of the Singapore Chefs Association during the Salut dinner. In an article from Hospitality Asia magazine's Nov./Jan. 2006 issue, the president mentor said:

I've worked with the different levels of staff from this organization for the past few years. I've found that their staff members are given proper training and product knowledge. They are definitely some of the best in the business. They're very approachable and service oriented. The leaders of the company are supportive of the industry. They also know how to mix fun with business which is important in today's hectic life. I can only salute them for their professionalism.

At another function, the president of the Food and Beverage Association Singapore congratulated our team members. He said, "A big thank you to this wonderful team of energetic people who are very passionate in everything they do. I can see your commitment to service excellence. Evidently you have made the difference!"

> I can see your commitment to service excellence. Evidently you have made the difference!

We continued to articulate more MAD plans. One of them was honoring the national culinary team who won second place at a prestigious international competition. In her congratulatory speech to the national team, D. Lauren requested the team to rise up. This was followed by a television news clipping of Singapore's Prime Minister Lee Hsien Loong congratulating the national team for their great victory! Everyone was surprised! They applauded the team. We knew that our act had greatly inspired the team and the industry. We had made the difference! We were a MAD team!

The thing that separates us
from our competitors
is that we put our hearts and soul
into delighting our customers.
We create delightful experiences
for our customers to remember.
We build enduring and
memorable relationships
with our customers.
We prove to them that we
have them in our hearts.
We are their right
business partners.
Our customers recognize it
and reward us!

are you mad?

Conclusion

Important Points
To Remember

A Closing Note

IMPORTANT MAD POINTS
To remember

Your competitors may adopt the same plans and strategies that you have. They may have stronger brands than yours or have higher sales turnover than yours.

But what will ultimately determine the outcome of your plans and strategies is the way you execute them and the way you shape your approach to achieve the desired results.

You must define the method and style of your execution because the way you fashion your execution matters.

Your ability and depth of execution is the differentiation factor to the success of MADbiz.

One Last Note ...

I do not know anyone who has gotten to the top without hard work. That is the recipe.
— Margaret Thatcher

Making a difference in your work demands hard work. However, do not confuse hard work with the impossible. Hard work equals diligence, perseverance, tenacity, and patience. With passion, hard work becomes easier and exciting. Passion also breeds enthusiasm; it generates intensity in thought, purpose, and focus and drives your will power, helping you see beyond the hard work toward the end results you desire. Passion fuels energy you need to pursue your goals.

It is impossible to make a difference—this thought is closely tied to our natural tendency to reject or resist change. There are some who fear change. Change demands that we have the courage to discard old ways of thinking. Some cling on to their past; their own successes were valuable lessons in their time but no longer fit into the culture and climate of another organization. Some jealously guard their own jobs against any change for fear of losing their authority or position.

People who are always chanting, "No, it can't be done! It's not possible!" have a negative mental attitude (NMA). They are more inclined to reject new ideas and change. Often the root of their self-doubt and negativity comes from low confidence, a sense of insecurity, a lack of ability, and feelings of insignificance. Often these are based more on emotions and negative influences than reality. Then there are those who are overwhelmed by a fear of failure or a repetition of unpleasant or negative experiences.

Throw out that sense of negativity! Revive your spirit. Strengthen your soul. Renew your mind. Do not let it affect your well-being or let it prevent you from being MAD in your personal life, workplace, and marketplace.

Be simple but sharp in your plans, strategies, and execution. Eliminate complexity. In all, be consistent. Every action must reflect the purpose of your goal.

> **The secret of success is constancy of purpose.**
> — **Benjamin Disraeli**

Do not feel overwhelmed by MAD! Often we think that so many actions are required to accomplish MAD tasks or projects that it will result in our taking no action instead.

Be focused. Be objective. Do the things that need to be done to achieve your desired results, and focus on achieving the highest possible quality of results.

Remember, you have the power to shape the results you desire. Believe and work on it!

People avoid action often because
they are afraid of the consequences,
for action means risk and danger.
Danger seems terrible from a distance;
it is not so bad if you have a close look at it.
And often it is a pleasant companion,
adding to the zest and delight of life.

— Jawaharlal Nehru

are you mad?

Appendix

What is MADBiz?

The Bedrock of MADBiz

Execution Is Key in MADBiz

Strategic and Tactical Thrust
of MADBiz

What Is
MADBiz?

MADBiz is an integrated business program with a holistic approach.

MADBiz helps organizations create positive changes in culture and behavior in the workplace, directly impacting business results in their respective marketplace. MADBiz focuses on

- strengthening employees' morale and capability,

- building excellent customer relationships,

- maximizing and seizing business potential, and

- increasing business performance and profitability.

With an eye on delivering measurable results, **MADBiz** utilizes the power in focusing and shaping to achieve a desired end. Starting with the desired end results, it works backward (top down) to formulate strategies and programs that aim to translate business objectives and goals into **MADBiz** action plans.

The Bedrock
of
MADBiz

Goals and Strategies

- Lay a solid, workable foundation upon which to build your vision and goals.

- Integrate and align all plans, strategies, and points of differentiation with your objectives.

- Challenge the status quo. Set stretched but attainable expectations and measurements.

- Every plan and strategy must be results-focused.

- Consciously shape your plans to achieve the results you want.

- Stay focused on the goals. Do not be sidetracked by peripheral issues.

Don't ever be too impressed with goal setting.
Be impressed with goal getting!
— John Maxwell

Program Execution

- The transformation of ideas into actions must be bold, not mediocre.

- Execution of plans must be consistent, detailed, seamless, sharp, and reflective of the organization's vision and business objectives.

- Every initiative must come with purpose and targets.

- Every plan or program must communicate its intended message.

- Engage in creative thinking and outside-the-box ideas that provide solutions.

- All programs should generate excitement and meaning. They should be fun to work on and rewarding.

Customers

- In all, focus on winning the hearts and minds of your customers.

- Delight them with good, memorable experiences!

- Deliver not just what is required but what is desired.

- Be top-of-the-mind and core-of-the-heart of your customers.

Three-Pronged Relationship

- Nurture and develop sustainable "win-win-win" relationships between the organization, the staff, and the customers.

- Create a progressive mindset and a learning culture.

- Orchestrate high-performing teams to build the organization's capabilities.

- Every staff member is your ambassador!

- Your customers are your paymasters!

- Your organization, your staff members, and your customers are partners for success!

Execution Is Key
in
MADBiz

While goals and strategies are relatively easy to formulate, true success hinges primarily on effective implementation or execution. Many failures are the result of poor execution.

MADBiz thus focuses on creating dynamic and creative executions. An intense focus that allows one to see what is and not what there seems to be as well as consistency of purpose determines the outcome and shapes the desired results.

MADBiz involves a tenacious discipline in executing all programs in a way that deploys all available resources to draw out the maximum benefits while working in accordance with an organization's vision for its best long-term interests.

Strategic and Tactical Thrust of MADBiz

- Create
- Leverage
- Differentiate
- Dominate

Create

**The most effective way
to manage change
successfully is to create it.**
— Peter Drucker

Open your heart and mind to identify and think of ideas, concepts, plans, and solutions that you have never thought of or with which you are unfamiliar. Renovate your (old) way of thinking. Step out of the boundaries you have set. Move away from your fixed ways of doing things that contribute to mediocre performances. Do not limit your capabilities and potential.

Look outside yourself! Renew your perspective! Having the right perspective is critical in achieving your desired results. Think of this: *"What looks like a monster through a magnifying glass is only a harmless house spider to the naked eye."*

Realign your focus. When you have the wrong focus, you will be unable to see clearly. Your vision is blurred because your focus is not aligned with your vision. Place and fix your focus on the right target, the right track, and the right resources to reach your destination in record time.

Engage in creative thinking. Be innovative and think outside the box. Do not be afraid. Do not settle for the status quo. Challenge the norms, and take dramatic actions to reinforce the business's vision. Move forward with calculated risks. Every worthwhile idea comes with a risk. No risks often mean no real gains. Every new and courageous idea will have implications and consequences. It is up to you to turn them successfully into long-term benefits. Because they are new ideas or approaches, you therefore have the power and ability to shape their results. Size them up. Put in place plans and solutions that will effectively produce the results you desire. Be courageous!

Construct and fashion bold ideas into your plans. Set your spirit free to generate fresh ideas and work plans.

Create what you desire; you have the creative power to produce what you aim for.

Imagine—if you had the power to create, what would you create? If you could redeem your losses, what would you have done differently today? Whatever you want to do, do it now!

Leverage

**Leaders are those who make
the most of every moment,
of every opportunity,
and of every available resource.**
— Theodore Roosevelt

Tap on available resources and maximize them. Do not undermine or underestimate what you are and what you have now. Remember that at this stage, you have to make do with what you already have.

Often we overlook our talents, our capabilities, our resources, and the people around us. We look elsewhere, desperately seeking answers when what we need is right on our doorstep!

Look within and identify what you have now that you have not used to the max or have not fully taken advantage of to deliver the desired growth.

Spot patterns, trends, or issues that have an impact on your business. Once they have been identified, be decisive and employ the most appropriate strategies to eliminate them (if they obstruct the growth of your business) or ride on them (if they are positive impacts) to achieve your goals.

Do not be too reliant or contented with the current status or image or track record.

Deploy, maximize, and amplify the benefits of the best resources to meet your objectives. Use multiple methods or integrate resources and methods as the basis for deliberating strategies that will work to your advantage.

Use positive influences to gain support, cooperation, and commitment to grow your business agenda. Be humble, and seek support or obtain a buy-in to gain agreement.

In pursuing your goals, avoid relying on the power of your position or status. Do not seek success at the expense of others. Consider positive strategic partnerships or collaborations whenever necessary.

Belief and confidence will help you increase and multiply what you have now. Nothing you have now is too small to multiply. It is your own perception; if you think you have nothing worthwhile to work on, then you are right—you really have nothing. However, if you believe you have something that can grow, then things will be productive and reproduce according to their kind.

Differentiate

**A dwarf standing on the shoulders of a giant
may see farther than the giant himself.**
— Unknown

**Decide what you want to be and how you want your
customers to see and perceive you.** Then work toward this
identity. In this way, you can distinguish your strategies,
plans, solutions, and programs from your competitors.

Style and method of execution are also key points of
differentiation that can position you apart from the rest.

Know your positioning, know your substance, and know your
targeted customers' wants and desires. Identify and select an
area or aspect of business that will differentiate your business
from your competitors.

See change as a challenge and an opportunity to improve
and excel. Be receptive and positive toward change. Have
courage to change. Change energizes and stimulates the
mind and body. Change requires a paradigm shift into a
new way of thinking and doing. Change must come with a
purpose and the readiness to accept the consequences and
effects arising from the change.

Probe yourself:

- *What is so special about my business?*

- *Why should my customers come to me and not to my competitors?*

- *How and what do I want my customers to remember of me?*

- *What else can I do to ensure growth opportunities are realized?*

The answers to these questions will help you understand that which differentiates you from others.

Your points of differentiation can come from product attributes or solutions, brands, services, pricing, distribution or product accessibility, or creating customer experiences. These differentiations will set you apart from the competition and help you carve a slice of the market for yourself.

Focus on your point(s) of differentiation, and integrate all your work plans to reflect them. Do not conduct hit-and-run campaigns that do not strengthen the attributes of your point(s) of differentiation. Such short-sighted activities and programs are not enduring, and they cannot produce long-lasting results. Be consistent, and do not compromise the quality of your differentiation. Be diligent in following through all effects and initiatives of the differentiation. Work toward a distinctive edge of advantage.

Remember that all initiatives you embark on to differentiate yourself from your competitors must always have *consistency of purpose, and they must be in concert with your organization's vision.* If your customers perceive you as no different from your competitors, you will likely lose out in market share and risk being displaced!

To be the preferred supplier of your customers, you must stand out among all the other suppliers in your targeted market. In this, you must be prominent and distinctive in the eyes of your targeted customers, so be passionate in pursuing your growth plans. You must position yourself as the *top-of-the-mind and core-of-the-heart* among your customers and potential customers!

Dominate

**If I have seen a little further
it is by standing on the shoulders of giants.**
— Sir Isaac Newton

Focus on your differentiating points and strategize to lead in the targeted product categories, brands, segmentations, or channels.

Do not neglect your points of differentiation. Once you know what they are, you should work on *mastering* them. As you grow, they may even vary in response to changes in your customers' preferences or needs.

Dictate the market; do not be led. Be proactive. Never adopt the attitude of "Things can't get any worse!" Often circumstances become worse as a result of our indifference and negligence.

Complacency leads to procrastination. Act and move swiftly before your competitors surprise you! Reacting to a situation or a competitor's attack consumes more energy and resources than when you are being proactive. To remain in a dominating position, you must move faster than your competitors; you must preempt them. Do not open the door of your business to allow in events that will control or dictate you.

Never compromise on quality, be it with products, services, business programs, sales and marketing campaigns, distribution, etc. To be on top, to remain as market leader, and to dominate, never slack in or neglect the promises you make to your customers. You can easily gain a customer through trial purchase and lose a valued customer instantly, but to win a customer back takes up to ten times a normal selling effort because customers who perceive that their loyalty is not reciprocated or appreciated can easily feel betrayed. It is a very expensive lesson indeed when you lose a good customer.

Establish close communications with your customers. Constantly touch base with people who contribute to your business. You must know them! All stakeholders must feel that they have access to your organization.

Always keep a lookout for opportunities to improve the business and create major growth opportunities. Instill a learning culture and a positive working environment; inspire team leadership to create shared responsibility, and equip them to take charge and be accountable for building organizational capability and performance.

To keep your number-one position in the market, regular monitoring and progress and results reviews should be conducted against growth goals. Stretch expectations and measurements so they will drive high performance. Where there are grievances or disruptions within the organization (whether people, operations, or systems), do not delay in tackling them. Take ownership and responsibility by managing them. When necessary, take immediate action to eliminate or reduce any such negative or obstructive factors.

Remember the three Cs in a winning organization: character, competence, and connection. You must achieve a good balance of these three attributes. An employee who is highly competent but who does not possess good character is not worth keeping. He or she can be likened to a malignant cancer cell that will in no time spread and kill all the other good cells. A person of good character but with reasonable competence can be developed and trained to eventually take on greater responsibility. Among the key qualities of someone with good character are humility, integrity, diligence, faithfulness, and a readiness to learn. He or she should also be passionate about the job and possess some wisdom. Everyone within the organization, especially leaders, should have healthy and good communications with internal and external customers while keeping him or herself abreast of developments, insights, and happenings on the ground. Remember, employees represent and are the faces and ambassadors of the organization.

Expand your vision, and view things as if you standing on a mountaintop. Do not lose sight of the bigger picture! Create entirely new internal and external concepts that will redefine your approach to the business.

Do not let short-term obstacles hinder you from pursuing your long-term goals. Make decisions that will set the ground for you to create the future you desire. The quality and timeliness of your decisions determine the success of your plans. Do not bask in your past glories or experiences and expect them to define your future!

Set challenging growth goals. Create, orchestrate, and promote the team to high standards of performance. Inspire and drive their commitment to high levels of growth. Do not demonstrate behavior or employ strategies and tactics that are contradictory or inconsistent with your vision. Exemplify your market leadership by mirroring values of the organization.

Remember that many market leaders fail or make mistakes in worthy projects because of impatience and lack of planning, preparation, and time. Be deliberate with your projects, ensuring that they are well thought of and properly executed. Stick to your plan. Be decisive, and do not make decisions as a result of pressure from others.

Be the best player in your targeted market or category. Be the most efficient in living out your point(s) of differentiation. Be the most sought-after solution provider to your customers.

Ask yourself these questions constantly:

What should I do now to be in the dominant position?

How should I operate my business to keep the leading edge?

What sacrifices or compromises should I make now in order to achieve my desired market share and position?

What other alternative plans and strategies must I adopt to further expand my market-leading position?

are you mad?

Stay MAD to make a difference in your workplace and marketplace by keeping in touch with updates on how to build and sustain a MAD Culture at www.madbiz.org.

Interact with the author and get involved in the activities as we create a MAD world together!

About the Author

If there is one word to describe D.Lauren, it can be no other but MAD. Throughout her career, her peers, subordinates and superiors have always been taken aback by her penchant for doing things differently. Some even labeled as MAD.

At first, it had been accompanied by a fair share of skepticism. But over time, they had called her MAD with more than a touch of admiration. From being dismissed as "impossible" and "a bridge too far", her radical concepts and revolutionary initiatives are now accepted and embraced as inspiring and innovative. She has gone the distance to show that being different and, of course, being a little MAD can be a powerful asset.

Today, D.Lauren is a coach for team leadership and managing organizational change as well as a consultant for brand building and creating customer experiences. She brings with her decades of brand management and leadership experience in four major industries, having started out in a publishing firm before moving on to multinational corporations like Scott Paper (now known as Kimberly Clark), Silverstone Tyres and finally heading the national operations of a Fortune Global 500 organization. In this last post, D.Lauren was one of the youngest country managing directors of Unilever.

A frequent traveler, D.Lauren now lives in Australia with her husband and daughter. She is also an author of several spiritual and inspirational books.

Another Book by the Author

MAD in Action is the second book in a series first introduced by MADBiz - The MAD Culture on making a difference in the workplace and marketplace. Whereas the first book shared with readers the broad concept of changing the way we think and act to generate better results, this book dives into the details with practical examples of harnessing MAD to enrich our personal and professional lives as well as those around us.

This book presents the execution of MAD in all its mad glory. The book is a pictorial celebration of why, how and what we must do to transform ourselves and become an agent of change in both our work and market places.

Containing more than 100 illustrations and graphics, MAD in Action is a fun read and visual feast that can take the reader over the edge to become MAD!

www.ingramcontent.com/pod-product-compliance
Lightning Source LLC
Chambersburg PA
CBHW032003170526
45157CB00002B/521